BUILDING TRUST
for
Better Schools

BUILDING TRUST

for

Better Schools

Research-Based Practices

Julie Reed Kochanek

Foreword by Anthony Bryk

CORWIN PRESS
A SAGE Publications Company
Thousand Oaks, California

For information:

Corwin Press
A Sage Publications Company
2455 Teller Road
Thousand Oaks, California 91320
www.corwinpress.com

Sage Publications Ltd.
1 Oliver's Yard
55 City Road
London EC1Y 1SP
United Kingdom

Sage Publications India Pvt. Ltd.
B-42, Panchsheel Enclave
Post Box 4109
New Delhi 110 017 India

Printed in the United States of America

Library of Congress Cataloging-in-Publication Data

Kochanek, Julie Reed.
Building trust for better schools: Research-based practices / by Julie Reed Kochanek.
   p. cm.
Includes bibliographical references and index.
ISBN 1-4129-1513-9 (cloth)—ISBN 1-4129-1514-7 (pbk.)
   1. School improvement programs—United States—Case studies. 2. Educational leadership—United States—Case studies. 3. School management and organization—United States—Case studies. I. Title.
LB2822.82.K63 2005
371.2'00973—dc22

2004025338

This book is printed on acid-free paper.

05 06 07 08 09 10 9 8 7 6 5 4 3 2 1

Acquisitions Editor:	Elizabeth Brenkus
Editorial Assistant:	Candice L. Ling
Production Editor:	Melanie Birdsall
Copy Editor:	Cheryl Duksta
Typesetter:	C&M Digitals (P) Ltd.
Proofreader:	Teresa Herlinger
Indexer:	Kathy Paparchontis
Cover Designer:	Lisa Miller

For my daughters, Isabel and Sophie

Contents

Foreword

As Barbara Schneider and I brought to a close our decade-long study that culminated in *Trust in Schools* (Bryk & Schneider, 2002), we sought to test out our draft ideas against the critical reactions of colleagues. We looked to other scholars to critique our theoretical framework of trust as social resource for collective action, to scrutinize our overall methodology, and to offer plausible alternative explanations for the evidence that we had assembled. Similarly, we sought occasions to present our conceptual framework and core findings to diverse practitioner audiences, including school principals, teachers, and central office leaders. Our aim in *Trust in Schools* was to develop an empirically grounded theory of practice. A critical test in this regard was whether these ideas found salience among diverse groups of school practitioners. Quite simply, did our emerging understandings about relational trust help them think better about the improvement work in which they were involved?

While the reactions of both academic colleagues and school practitioners to *Trust in Schools* were generally quite positive, many of these early reviewers—especially practitioners—invariably asked a question for which we did not have an answer. These questions typically took the following form: "So I understand now that trust functions as an important resource for school improvement, but what do we know about how to develop such trust that I can use in direct work with a school community?" It is in seeking a response to this core question of practice improvement that the investigation reported on by Julie Kochanek in this book took root.

Although this is a short book, it is ambitious in its goal—to offer an empirically grounded theory of practice improvement. Our field is now rich with accounts of outstanding schools (call this "condition B") as well as critical commentary about the weak state of practices commonly found in many other schools (call this "condition A"). Good evidence, however, about how one might best navigate from "A" to "B" is much harder to secure. To date, we have had to rely mostly on retrospective accounts of successful school changes and more general clinical commentaries about school improvement practice.

Kochanek brings disciplined inquiry to this problem. She synthesizes concepts from a variety of literatures searching for clues—discerned in prior investigations in other applied fields—about the core processes involved in building trust. She then proceeds to delve deeper into these insights using both in-depth case studies and large-scale survey analyses from more than 400 school communities engaged in reform efforts during the late 1990s. *Building Trust for Better Schools* weaves together a complex tapestry of argument and evidence in specifying, testing, and refining an integrated set of propositions about effective trust building and the contextual features that shape these developments in varied school communities.

Along the way, Kochanek offers some provocative findings. Like many previous professional accounts, she documents the value of shared local school governance as a basis for trust formation among school professionals. She also, however, offers new evidence that the success of such arrangements is contingent on the base level of relational trust present in a school community. Absent at least some modicum of social resources to start with, a naïve effort to implement shared governance, rather than enhancing trust, could easily produce the opposite effect.

In a related vein, Kochanek documents that inclusive, facilitative leadership—another common feature in many professional accounts of good schools—can contribute powerfully to trust formation. However, she also documents that the deliberate use of formal role authority can likewise enable trust. Specifically, she describes how principals' efforts to counsel weak teachers contribute to trust building. To be sure, this strategy, if arbitrarily employed, would quickly eviscerate trust between teachers and their principal. When used thoughtfully as a last resort with teachers whose classroom practices are deeply problematic and who have clearly resisted improvement efforts, such actions demonstrate a principal's resolve to act in the best interest of children. Others in a school community quickly take notice and value leaders who are willing to take on the hard and sometimes painful tasks necessary to advance teaching and learning for every child. These are essential discernments about the integrity of leadership, which in turn fuel wider school–community trust building.

These accounts by Kochanek illuminate a fundamental confusion in much of the writings about school reform—conflating a desired end state with effective and necessary mechanisms for achieving it. While accounts of "condition B"—for example, school-based professional communities anchored in shared norms and with strong collegial accountability—can be very compelling, the necessary processes for getting to this state may be far from collegial.

On balance, some may well disagree with Kochanek's findings, and others may offer alternative explanations for the body of evidence documented in the pages that follow. This is precisely what a book like this should do—catalyze more informed, evidence-based conversations about the improvement of school practice. As Kochanek herself notes in her concluding chapter, this volume represents a first sketch of an interrelated set of school practices conducive to building trust. Much work remains on expanding these accounts and further testing these ideas through the day-to-day efforts at improving the organization and operation of our nation's schools. *Building Trust for Better Schools* now offers us new guidance for these next steps.

—Anthony Bryk
Stanford University

Preface

In recent research, trust has been shown to be a key resource in school reform. Increasing trust in schools has been linked to increased participation among faculty in school reform efforts, greater openness to innovations among teachers, increased outreach to parents, and even higher academic productivity in a school. While trusting relationships are not a substitute for student-centered, academically challenging instruction or a more participatory governance structure, they can be seen as the groundwork necessary for such interventions to succeed schoolwide. For example, a more rigorous curriculum that calls for changes in teaching methods is more likely to be adopted by the entire faculty and implemented in the intended fashion in a school where teachers trust one another and their principal. Similarly, trusting relationships among parents, teachers, and administrators allow shared decision making to work toward the benefit of the students rather than dissipating into conflict and personal agendas.

While the importance of trust in schools has been established, the key question posed by both researchers and school professionals remains: How is trust built among adults in elementary schools? This question is the primary focus of this book. My interest in issues of trust building evolved as I worked with Bryk and Schneider on their recent monograph, *Trust in Schools* (2002). Although their work focused on defining the components and benefits of trust in schools, their monograph concludes with a brief discussion of trust building and calls for further investigation of the process of developing trust in schools. As we worked on the monograph, we forced ourselves to concentrate on honing the elements of the theory of trust and our analysis of what trust could mean to a school's productivity. However, inevitably we asked ourselves how the schools we noted in our analysis that went from low to high trust over the course of three years were able to accomplish this change. If a new principal enters a low-trust school, what can be done to promote the development of high-trust relationships? It is from these discussions that this work emerged.

I began to develop a theory of trust building by relying on the literature on trust in organizations and linking it to the Bryk and Schneider (2002) conceptualization of trust in schools. I then turned to the literature on principal leadership and school change to bring specificity to the model in the context of schooling. After a look at why trust in schools is important in Chapter 1, my model for building trust and the literature that supports it are presented in Chapter 2. In an attempt to bring definition to the particularities of the model as it may be witnessed in the day-to-day work of the school, three semihistorical case studies of schools that have experienced a change in principal leadership and positive changes in relational trust are presented in Chapters 3, 4, and 5. Using survey data from teachers and principals in Chicago public schools, in Chapter 6 I test several hypotheses about trust building derived from the case study research. Finally, Chapter 7 sets out a discussion of the ramifications of this study on trust building—what the results tell us and how they might be applied to schools today.

Chicago public schools served as an interesting backdrop to this study on trust building in that they were in the midst of a major school reform effort for the time period studied. Legislation passed in the late 1980s created a local school council (LSC) for each public school; each LSC had control over any discretionary funds and had the power to hire or fire principals every four years. These LSCs consisted of two teachers, who were elected by the faculty, and six parents and two community members, who were elected by the community. The legislation also granted more autonomy for school principals as it reduced the power of the central office and gave principals the ability to hire faculty without regard to seniority rules. This decentralization of power made social relations between school professionals and the community even more important than in traditional school districts.

The dramatic changes in the power structure in Chicago public schools attracted a wealth of resources to both guide and study the phenomenon. Many researchers and members of local community agencies organized seminars to help train LSC members, created leadership networks for principals to explore their new roles, and obtained funding to study the efficacy of this form of school governance. In some cases, these professionals became partners with the central office, providing training and research services as independent contractors. Other groups received outside grants from foundations and maintained more distance from the formal structure.

Soon after the implementation of the reform began in 1989, Tony Bryk formed the Consortium on Chicago School Research (the Consortium) at the University of Chicago to study it. Backed by foundation grants, the Consortium brings together researchers and policy advocates who are concerned about urban education to investigate policy changes in the Chicago school system with the goal of informing future decision making. Founded in 1990, the Consortium conducted its first major survey of teachers and students in Chicago public schools in 1991. Topics covered in the survey included school governance, school leadership, instructional practices, professional development, professional communities, student engagement, parent involvement, opportunities to learn, and the school environment. Similar surveys were conducted in 1994, 1997, and 1999. Data from these surveys allowed Bryk and Schneider to develop school-level measures of teacher-teacher trust, teacher-principal trust, and teacher-parent trust. Along with this unique dataset, the Consortium has amassed data from the Chicago public school database, including student test score files, administrative records, and school-level demographic information, and combined it with U.S. Census data and several other datasets collected from public agencies. The work in this book relies heavily on the data resources of the Consortium. Their rich collection of data allowed me to identify schools for in-depth case study work and to empirically test the propositions coming from my model of trust building.

Acknowledgments

This book began as my dissertation at the University of Chicago. As such, I owe a great debt to my advisors, Tony Bryk, Barbara Schneider, and Charles Bidwell, for their guidance in the planning, implementation, and analysis of the study. I am especially grateful to Tony for his time and support over the years as I trained to be a researcher at the University of Chicago. Indeed, much of my interest in trust in schools developed under the tutelage of Tony and Barbara as I worked with them on their study of relational trust, and it is through the encouragement of both Tony and Charles that this book came to be published.

For their impressive collection of data and pursuit of better measurement, I must thank the staff at the Consortium on Chicago School Research. The quantitative analyses and the selection of case study schools in this book were possible in large part due to their many years of research and analysis. In particular, I must acknowledge the team of data analysts with whom I worked at the Consortium: John Easton, Stuart Luppescu, Elaine Allensworth, Shazia Miller, Matt Gladden, Jenny Nagaoka, and Todd Rosenkrantz. I benefited greatly from their knowledge of schools, data collection, and statistical analysis as well as their friendship and moral support.

The process of turning a dissertation into a book manuscript takes time, not only for the hours of rewriting and reorganization but also for the change in mindset from pupil to academic. For their financial support, which gave me the time to make this transition, I want to thank the Center for Research on Educational Opportunity at the University of Notre Dame, especially Maureen Hallinan and David Sikkink. During my year at Notre Dame as a postdoctoral fellow, I enjoyed the motivation provided by my fellow RISE members, the refreshing look at the trust literature from my students, and the friendly support of Sylvia Phillips.

Needless to say, this book and the study it describes would not have been possible without the participation of the principals and teachers at MacNeil, Mills, and Cole Magnet elementary schools. These busy school professionals granted me access to their schools, notified me of special events and meetings, and gave up personal time to talk with me about a subject that isn't always easy—relationships. I appreciate their candor and thoughtfulness that led to the insights in this book.

Finally, I would like to thank my husband, Jeff Kochanek, and my children, Isabel and Sophie, for their emotional support throughout the implementation of this study and the development of this book. They inspire me to continue to work toward better schools and reassure me when I realize the work that lies ahead.

PUBLISHER'S ACKNOWLEDGMENTS

The author and Corwin Press gratefully acknowledge the contributions of the following individuals:

Kermit Buckner, Professor
Chair, Department of Educational
  Leadership
East Carolina University,
  College of Education
Greenville, NC

Harriet Gould, Principal
Raymond Central Elementary
  Schools
Valparaiso, NE

David Hulsey, Assistant Professor
University of West Georgia
Carrollton, GA

Carmen Manning, Assistant
  Professor
Department of English
University of Wisconsin–Eau Claire
Eau Claire, WI

Ann Porter, Principal
Lewis and Clark Elementary
  School
Grand Forks, ND

Barbara Schneider, Professor
  of Sociology
University of Chicago
Chicago, IL

Joyce Uglow, Principal
Lyons Center School
Burlington, WI

Rosemary Young, Principal
President-Elect of NAESP
Watson Lane
  Elementary School
Louisville, KY

About the Author

Julie Reed Kochanek received her PhD from the University of Chicago in 2003. She is currently an assistant professor of sociology at Southern Oregon University in Ashland, Oregon.

1 Introduction

Making a Case for Trust

When we want others to cooperate with us, we can coerce them with threats of punishment, or we can entice them with promises of rewards. This punishment-reward system works well when we are able to tell whether or not others are cooperating with us. For example, in a typical outing to a family restaurant, we might witness some parents warning their children that if they do not behave in the restaurant, they will be going to bed early. We might see other parents compelling their children's good behavior with a promise of dessert after dinner. In this example, either system works fairly well, as the parents can easily judge whether or not their children have lived up to the bargain and either are free from punishment or merit their reward.

We experience many situations in which it is not so clear whether or not others are cooperating with us. In these cases, the punishment-reward system alone does not suffice. In taking the car to the mechanic, most of us are unable to assess if either the diagnosis of the problem or the proposed resolution is correct. To make matters worse, we realize that the mechanic has a significant monetary incentive to not cooperate fully with us and propose more work than is necessary. In such cases, we must form a trust relationship with others as part of our decision to interact with them. In the car mechanic example, we might initially choose to trust a mechanic based on a neighbor's recommendation, the appearance of the garage, or the personal attributes of the mechanic. If the initial outcome seems positive, we might eventually build trust based on knowledge of the mechanic's past behavior, and concerns about potential rewards and punishments become less important when deciding whether or not to leave our car in the mechanic's care.

WHY IS TRUST IN SCHOOLS SO IMPORTANT?

The role of trust between a car mechanic and his or her customer is similar to that of trust between school professionals and parents. Most parents lack the knowledge necessary to judge if a teacher is doing his or her job well. Even if they did have training in child development and pedagogy, most parents are unable to spend a significant amount of time in the classroom to truly evaluate a teacher. Instead, parents entrust their children to teachers and principals based on recommendations, the appearance of the school, and, sometimes, the appearance of the teacher or principal. Over the course of the academic year, parents may place their trust based on successful interactions with their child's teacher or student outcomes that indicate to them that the teacher must be doing a good job.

While the car mechanic example works pretty well, there are some important differences between garages and schools with regard to trust. As Bidwell (1970) noted when comparing doctors and teachers, normally the bond between the professional and the client is a voluntary, one-on-one bond that involves a fee for service. In schools, however, students enter on an involuntary basis, teachers work as single professionals interacting with dozens of students at once, and the clients receive the services for free (in the case of public education).

Bidwell (1970) argues that the special organizational properties of the school as a client-serving organization have implications for the formation of a trust relationship between professional and client. The involuntary nature of schooling constrains the options of students and teachers in forming professional relationships. If a patient does not trust his or her doctor, the patient may choose another. However, a student is placed in a classroom—and often even a school—without a choice. If the student does not trust the ability of the teacher, the student has few options. Because the student cannot easily move to another classroom or school the most readily available alternative is to remain in the classroom but withdraw cooperation and support. The teacher also suffers in this example by having to cope with a student who does not trust the teacher's abilities and is therefore not cooperative.

The issue of judging competence that was highlighted in the car mechanic example is even more severe in schooling. As noted by Bryk and Schneider (2002) in *Trust in Schools*, the goals of schooling are far reaching and not easily agreed on. Whereas the car mechanic is expected to keep the car running smoothly, some parents expect schools to teach academic knowledge solely, while others also expect schools to promote certain value systems and develop cultural awareness. Business leaders want schools to produce good workers, while community members expect schools to produce good citizens. While expectations vary, there is little open discussion or debate within communities about what should be the aims of schooling and how schools might accomplish them.

Bryk and Schneider (2002) further assert that even if the aims of schooling were defined and agreed on, there is no consensus among school professionals on how to produce them. Extensive research on effective instruction has not produced a professional knowledge base that dictates specific teaching practices for specific outcomes. Neither instructional methods nor curricula have uniformly been successful in producing increased academic knowledge or improving students' character development. The authors argue that even if best practices were identified, it would be difficult to enforce their use throughout the school since the organization of schools prevents parents and even administrators from effectively monitoring teaching practices. This leaves principals and fellow teachers in a similar situation to parents. Classroom visits can be made for periodic monitoring. However, teachers cannot be constantly observed or assessed to ensure that they are following a specific instructional plan.

In research on organizational structure, the lack of agreement on organizational goals and the inability of management to judge whether or not workers are doing their jobs lead the organization to separate performance from outcomes, or to decouple (Meyer & Rowan, 1977). Rather than judging an individual's performance based on a set of outcomes, organizations under these conditions develop expectations for behavior. If individuals meet these expectations for behavior, they are thought to be doing their job. Meyer and Rowan call these expectations for behavior institutionalized myths. They argue that America's schools are filled with examples of institutionalized myths. We expect schools to be divided into classrooms, with one teacher assigned to a group of twenty to thirty students. We expect teachers to maintain authority and discipline in the classroom. When we see students respond in an orderly fashion to their teacher as we pass in the hallway, we think that that teacher probably is doing a good job.

When performance is separated from assessment of outcomes and instead we look for individuals and organizations to meet our traditional expectations for behavior, organizations are said to be operating under a logic of confidence—that is, people have faith that others are doing what they are supposed to be doing. In an atmosphere where adequate performance is assumed rather than verifiable, degrees of competence are not discernable, and only gross incompetence is detected. Thus, parents assume that teachers are doing what they can to produce learning in their children. Teachers assume that their colleagues are acting appropriately behind classroom doors. Without evidence to the contrary, the school continues to operate with legitimacy.

As one might expect, there are problems with maintaining an organization in this decoupled state where we assume people are doing their jobs and the only evidence we have to support our assumptions is that they are meeting a traditional set of expectations for behavior that go along with their role. First and most obvious, people might not be doing their jobs. A fourth-grade teacher might suspect that her colleague teaching third grade did not adequately prepare her students to advance, but, without evidence of gross incompetence, it is difficult to confirm those suspicions. Second, the institutionalized myths set a minimum level of competence in defining behaviors for a job. There is no focus on how to do the job well. The myths about teachers set minimum standards for orderliness and cleanliness rather than promoting a standard of dedicated teaching. Finally, traditional myths or expectations for behavior are slow to change and stand in the way of adaptations that might make teaching and learning more efficient and effective.

EFFICIENT SCHOOLS AS NETWORK ORGANIZATIONS

The traditional organization of schooling itself is an institutionalized myth that slows innovations that might lead to greater efficiency. Schools are usually structured as bureaucracies, with commonly understood roles for state boards and superintendents, local boards and superintendents, principals, and teachers. In fact, economic theory predicts that schools should operate best as bureaucracies precisely because they operate with competing goals, and it is difficult to evaluate individual performance (Ouchi, 1980).

However, other organizational conditions of schooling indicate that schools might operate more efficiently as networks rather than bureaucracies if members of a school community were able to openly define a set of goals. In organizational theory, networks are defined as loosely grouped entities that are dependent on one another for resources and information to create one final product. Networks are particularly useful when there is a need for reliable information and when outcomes are not easily measured (Powell, 1990).

Networks operate under a set of norms or standards for behavior that support working toward mutual goals and forsaking individual goals that might come in conflict with the mutual goal. Members of a network agree to give to others with an expectation that at some future date they will receive a benefit from a member of the network. While they all work toward a common goal that will benefit each individually, members agree not to pursue their own interests if it will hurt others in the network. Such norms of behavior in a network increase everyone's sense of security to enhance the spread of information, allow for added risk taking, and bring together new combinations of approaches.

As discussed earlier, the outcomes of schooling are difficult to measure. In addition, dependencies exist across role relationships in all schools. Teachers are dependent on one another as children are passed from one grade to the next and must build on the knowledge learned in past years. Parents are dependent on teachers to educate their children appropriately. Teachers are dependent on principals to create school conditions that are conducive to helping children learn.

In addition to the interdependencies, there is a need for efficient sharing of information in schools across role relationships. Parents and teachers who share information on the children can more easily meet the needs of individual children. With efficient communication, parents can better prepare their children for school and work with their children at home. Teachers who communicate with parents may learn how to better bridge any gap in cultures between home and school.

Effective schools research has described schools that successfully operate as networks (Bryk & Schneider, 1996; Meier, 1995, 2002; Spillane & Thompson, 1997). In these schools, goals are openly discussed and agreed on, and the adults in the school community are willing to subjugate their own personal needs to do what is best for the children. In addition, these schools have incorporated collegial observation and discussions of professional standards into their daily operations to keep performance ambiguity low. These schools are deliberately challenging many of the institutionalized myths of schooling, such as the organization of classrooms, the measurement of student outcomes, and the isolation of teachers.

Of course, the stories of successful network schools emphasize the need to build trusting relationships. Some level of trust is necessary to begin discussions on important and heartfelt issues, such as the goals of the school. Higher levels of trust are needed to begin sharing information and resources with one another without knowing when or if repayment is coming. Teachers who invest significant amounts of their time helping their colleagues learn and master new instructional methods may have to wait years to see that investment pay off in higher achievement levels throughout the school. Finally, collegial observation and peer evaluation require an extremely high level of trust between teachers as they make themselves vulnerable to one another and invite criticism for learning purposes.

Trust is an especially useful tool for schools that are attempting to undertake large reform efforts. Trust can facilitate conversations about instructional reform that give the experts a chance to share their understanding of the reform with the teachers and teachers a chance to share their feedback on how the reality of the reform's implementation measures up to expectations (Spillane & Thompson, 1997). Teachers who report high levels of trust with their colleagues also express a greater openness to innovations (Bryk & Schneider, 1996). In trusting environments, teachers are able to push one another's thinking about instruction and schooling and the ways in which the reform could affect student learning.

Trust between the principal and faculty is particularly important for school reform. Teacher-principal trust allows the principal to introduce instructional and organizational changes to a more receptive faculty. Teachers who feel valued as professionals are open to input from a principal. Faculty members who report high levels of trust also describe a strong commitment among teachers to the school and a recognition among the faculty that they have a collective responsibility for the welfare of their students (Bryk & Schneider 1996). The latest research on trust in schools has even demonstrated a positive relationship between trust and school effectiveness, making a connection between the growth of trust and organizational changes, which can lead to improved educational outcomes for students (Bryk & Schneider, 2002; Goddard, Tschannen-Moran, & Hoy, 2001; Hoy, Tarter & Witkoskie, 1992).

HOW IS TRUST DEFINED IN SCHOOLS?

As the research continues to point to trust as being an important factor in schools, we should take some time to fully examine the concept to see what exactly trust looks like in the context of schooling. Two sets of researchers have persistently explored the operation of trust in schools as well as its benefits. Hoy and his colleagues (Goddard et al., 2001; Hoy et al., 1992; Hoy & Tschannen-Moran, 1999; Tarter, Bliss, & Hoy, 1989; Tarter, Sabo, & Hoy, 1995; Tschannen-Moran & Hoy, 1998) worked from a school climate perspective to develop a definition of trust in schools. From this perspective, trust exists as a characteristic of the school and is maintained as part of the school culture. Bryk and Schneider (1996, 2002) conceptualized trust in schools as a product of the everyday interactions that affect person-to-person relationships in the school. From their perspective, the trust formed between individuals can build to become part of the school culture as well as affect the structural characteristics of the school. Although these two sources of research developed simultaneously and separately, much of the work is parallel and the results are similar.

The body of work coming out of Ohio State University from Hoy and his colleagues (Tarter et al., 1989, p. 295) defines trust as a group understanding that both the group itself and the individuals within the group are reliable. Further conceptual study from this group led to a description of the five components of faculty trust: benevolence, reliability, competence, honesty, and openness (Hoy & Tschannen-Moran, 1999). *Benevolence* is defined as confidence in the goodwill of others. *Reliability* is the idea that someone can be counted on to come through, and *competence* is the ability to come through. *Honesty* is a global concept for one's character and includes acting in accordance with what one says, accepting responsibility for one's actions, avoiding manipulative behavior, and behaving consistently. Finally, *openness* is the degree to which information is freely shared across parties.

The Bryk and Schneider (2002) work on trust conceptualizes trust in schools as being formed around the specific roles that people play in this setting. Adults in schools interact as parents, teachers, and principals. Each person has an understanding about their own obligations in playing their role and expectations about the role obligations of the other adults in the school. The growth of trust depends in part on the degree to which people have shared understandings of their role obligations. However, because there is not open discussion about what is expected from each other, people use less direct methods to assess each others' fulfillment of role obligations. Typically, people look for actions that conform to their expectations of the role. We think of a good teacher as being attentive to students' needs, using sound pedagogy, and being dedicated to the students' development. However, we don't often witness enough interactions between teachers and students to assess whether or not a teacher is meeting these expectations. Even if we did have full access to all teacher-student interaction, it would be difficult to assess whether or not a teacher meets our criteria for a good teacher. Because we lack information and experience ambiguity in our expectations, people often use a process of discerning the intentions that motivate others when deciding whether or not an individual conforms to their expectations. For example, parents do not always have direct access to their child's classroom. Therefore, they cannot monitor the daily efforts of the teacher on their child's behalf. However, they can make a judgment that this teacher appears dedicated to doing whatever he or she can to benefit the children in the classroom. As such, parents might feel that the teacher meets their expectations of the role obligations of a teacher.

According to this conceptualization of trust, we typically use four key elements to discern the intentions of others in schools: respect, competence, integrity, and personal regard for others. *Respect* involves a basic regard for the dignity and worth of others. In respect that leads to trust, people listen to what others have to say and respond to it in some fashion. As with the Hoy literature (Goddard et al., 2001; Hoy et al., 1992;

Hoy & Tschannen-Moran, 1999; Tarter, Bliss, & Hoy, 1989; Tarter, Sabo, & Hoy, 1995; Tschannen-Moran & Hoy, 1998), *competence* is the ability to carry out the formal responsibilities of the role. However, Bryk and Schneider (2002) note that in schools competence is difficult to judge in some role relationships. For example, a teacher's competence cannot be directly assessed. Therefore, one cannot always note the differences between an average teacher and a good teacher. However, teaching incompetence is discernible through student scores and evaluation of practices. The authors also note that principal competence is more directly discernible by assessing outcomes, such as the upkeep of the school building and the orderliness of the school. *Integrity* is demonstrated by espousing beliefs that are based on doing what is in the best interests of the children and carrying through with actions that are consistent with those beliefs. This is similar to the Hoy construct of honesty. Finally, *personal regard* involves the display of intentions and behaviors that go beyond the formal requirements of the role.

Bryk and Schneider (2002) argue that role relationships in schools and the accompanying discernments are colored by the structure of power between the roles. The most obvious authority structure is between the principal and teacher in which the principal has formal power over the teacher in the form of hiring and firing, job evaluation, and resource allocation. The relationship between parents and school professionals also is affected by a power structure, although this structure varies in direction according to school location. Most urban schools display a pattern of the school professional having power over poor, less educated parents.

Despite these power structures, all participants remain dependent on one another to maintain or increase school productivity. Principals depend on teachers to provide high-quality classroom instruction for the students. Teachers depend on parents to support their efforts through homework supervision; supplemental enrichment activities; and the provision of basic needs such as proper nutrition, clothing, and hygiene. Parents depend on school professionals to educate their children and keep them safe. These mutual dependencies create feelings of vulnerability for all participants. Efforts to reduce these feelings of vulnerability can help to build trust.

WHAT DO WE KNOW ABOUT BUILDING TRUST?

While little attention has been given to the process of building trust among adults in a school community, there is research in organizational theory on the foundations of trust. The majority of this research presents factors that contribute to trust development, such as social similarity, proxies, contracts, and repeated interactions. This research often portrays trust as based on one concept or another, rather than viewing it as a growth process. An examination of the individual factors provides an understanding of possible paths to trust building in schools.

Social Similarity as a Predisposition to Trust

People often decide to place their trust with those who share physical and social similarities with them (Zucker, 1986). Immigrants coming to America in the late 1800s and early 1900s chose to live and work among people from the same country of origin, creating ethnic enclaves in major cities that survive even today. Swedes, for example, interacting mostly with other Swedes, felt reassured that by placing their trust with someone from the same culture they were less likely to be cheated. Their belief was that the shared culture would also mean that they had a shared value system and perhaps even be a little more likely to want to support each other. In general, it was a safer bet.

Even now, we often ascribe similar values and motivations to others who look like us or live in a similar fashion. Physical or social characteristics such as race, religion, or even the type of car a person drives are used to represent characteristics that are more difficult to predict or measure, such as competence, honesty, or kindness. For example, suppose we did indeed find ourselves in need of a car mechanic. Unhappy with the work done previously at another garage, we decide to try the new garage on the corner. The mechanic examines the car and informs us that we need an entirely new brake system. Nervous about spending so much money and about the prospect of continuing to drive with a faulty brake system, we notice a religious poster in the shop window. In asking the mechanic about it, we realize that he is a member of the church we attend. We reason that such a religious man must surely practice honesty and compassion in conducting his daily business, and, therefore, he must be less likely to cheat us. So we agree to have the brake system replaced.

The use of social similarity in placing trust can be seen today in schooling when parents and community members call for more African American teachers to serve in African American communities and Hispanic educators to teach in predominantly Hispanic schools. Although people may be predisposed to trust one another on the basis of social similarity, trust will not grow if it is not validated by subsequent actions. Unless social similarity is accompanied by respect, competence, integrity, and personal regard, the initial bond created by social and physical characteristics will fade away. Indeed, as parents and community members were given control over hiring the school principals in Chicago in the early 1990s, many White, male principals at minority schools were replaced with African Americans and Hispanics. However, just as Wong (1990) found that minority political representation did not necessarily benefit the minority populace, principals of the same race as the community being served did not guarantee good relationships within the school or increased student achievement. While social similarity may lend a principal an initial grace period of goodwill, alone it will not sustain the growth of trusting relationships.

The Limitations of Contracts in Establishing Trust

Some organizational theorists talk of contracts as a basis for trust to form among people in organizations (Batenburg, Raub, & Snijders, 1997; Gulati, 1995; Okun, 1981). Contracts often help people feel more secure because they spell out each person's obligations and assignments, the expected outcomes, and the compensation or punishment should the outcomes not be reached. Typically, contracts are more specific and narrow when made for one-time or short-term transactions, such as a sale of goods. However, when an exchange requires long-term or repeated interactions, contracts are less specific and more dependent on the relationship and are therefore more subjective (Macneil, 1985). In either case, contracts are believed to help individuals trust one another mainly because they provide a shared understanding of what is expected, and the parties fear the punishment should they not follow through.

While contracts may indeed ease the vulnerabilities people experience when interacting with others, they are limited in their power to build trust. As in the case of parents using punishments and rewards to coerce good behavior from their children, contracts are useful when outcomes are easily measured. When a librarian submits a book order to a publisher, she can recognize when that order has been filled correctly. However, as contracts become more open ended and subjective, they rely more on individual interpretations of the terms, and feedback is required to bring more definition to those terms (Rousseau & Parks, 1992). For example, a local grocer whose son has left town for college suddenly finds himself in need of help at the store. He places an ad for a cashier and soon hires a teenage boy to work after school. The boy believes that his job responsibilities are indicated by the job title. That is, he expects to attend to customers at the counter, ring up their orders, and put their goods in a bag. The grocer also envisions these duties as the main focus of the boy's job. However, he also expects that the boy will take his son's place at the store, lending a hand whenever possible. Initially, as the grocer and the boy are interpreting the job responsibilities differently, the grocer will have to ask the boy to help stock shelves, keep the windows and display cases clean, and answer the phone just as his son once did. Eventually the boy will catch on and reshape his definition of the job to include helping the grocer in whatever way possible. In this case, the employment contract as represented by the ad for cashier no longer operates in its original form but has become a social construction shared by both the grocer and the boy.

Most public school teachers in America fall under union representation and are therefore governed by contracts. These contracts often specify the number of hours teachers are expected to remain in the school each day, the number of professional development hours they are expected to put in, and any additional duties they are expected to complete outside of the normal working day. While these contracts can protect teachers from overwhelming demands on their time, they do not serve to ensure good teaching or effective schools.

Good teaching is a demanding task that is not often limited to the number of hours spent in the classroom. Teachers must spend extra time grading papers, preparing activities for the next day's classes, decorating the classroom, and learning new instructional techniques. In addition, the needs of individual children and their families do not always fall within the hours designated by a union contract. Teachers often spend their personal time either in the school or at home making phone calls and meeting with parents to create a better understanding of what an individual child needs to achieve. Beyond time, many dedicated teachers spend their own money on supplies, learning activities, and decorations to enhance their classroom's learning beyond the designated curriculum.

Even if these circumstances and extra efforts could be better specified in a contract, basing trust on contracts does not work well for schooling (Bryk & Schneider, 2002). As discussed earlier, schools typically work toward a wide range of goals, most of which have not been clearly agreed on by school professionals, parents, or community members. Even if the goals were clearly set, the outcomes are not easily measured. We continue to debate today how best to measure academic achievement. The measurement of other goals, such as character development, would prove even more arduous. Good teaching, the role of the school in character development, and the obligations of teachers and principals to their students are determined by individual social understandings of schooling. These individual understandings must be shared and transmitted through group norms and social cues expressed in everyday interactions among individuals. By agreeing on these obligations, participants in a school community can better fulfill one another's expectations and in doing so form trusting relationships.

The Inefficiency of Trust Based on Social Symbols

Trust might also be based on a socially acknowledged symbol or proxy that implies trustworthiness. This symbol might come in the form of an occupational role or certification process. For example, people trust priests to maintain confidentiality and act in a benevolent manner toward them based on their knowledge of the occupation rather than their personal knowledge of the priest himself. Businesses hire accounting firms to audit their financial statements to reassure investors that the current management is indeed trustworthy.

This type of trust, often called institutional-based trust, is the least efficient method of maintaining a society (Zucker, 1986). The symbols used to encourage the growth of trust must remain highly correlated with the desired qualities they represent. Otherwise, they will be discounted. For example, the failure of employees of the auditing firm of Arthur Andersen to either recognize or report suspect activities of a client, Enron, caused the collapse of the entire firm as its accreditation was no longer credible. Transactions based on this type of trust are generally dependent on the accepted organizational structure, whether or not it remains the most efficient. Therefore, in this system, the production of trust has extra costs associated with it.

Typically, schools receive a certain amount of trust by proxy from parents and community members. Parents entrust their children to school professionals for about six hours per day and, barring any displays of incompetence, accept that their children are well cared for and learning appropriately. However, the amount of trust given by proxy varies with the culture of the parent group (Lareau, 1989; Valdes, 1996). Research has noted that working-class parents are more likely to trust school professionals based on their credentials and assume that they are doing the job of educating the children. In addition, Hispanic cultures have been noted to defer to teachers and principals in matters of education more often than other ethnic groups in America. In both cases where trust relationships between parents and school professionals are based on the proxy of the occupational title, the parents were found to take a smaller or less active role in their child's education. This lack of parental involvement was noted as a factor in inferior educational outcomes, thereby demonstrating the inefficiency of trust by proxy.

Repeated Social Exchanges Support the Growth of Trust

Social similarity, contracts, and proxies may all be usurped by repeated interactions when examining trust relations. As noted previously, the initial bond created by social similarity must be supported once interaction has begun for trust to grow. Long-term contracts are influenced by the social relationships that develop around them in repeated interactions. Although a social symbol may be useful when outcomes are immediate and tangible, such as an exchange of money or goods, trust by proxy is not an effective means of achieving better educational outcomes. Rather, the teaming that is necessary between parent and school professional to produce higher learning outcomes is better sustained by trust developed through repeated social exchanges.

In a discussion of trust formation among mushroom collectors, Fine and Holyfield (1996) note that while novice collectors initially demonstrate trust based on the proxy of organizational position, they later trust individuals in the group based on their experience with them. When novices enter the organization, they participate in group activities that include cooking and eating the yield of a day's collecting. Here, they are willingly putting their lives in the hands of the group's expert, who must identify and remove any poisonous species. However, as members acquire experience with a group of collectors, they place trust in their colleagues based on displayed competence. Thus, the trust base moves from a proxy form to a base of repeated interaction.

Participants in a school community may experience a similar transition. Many parents entrust their children to school professionals due to their general trust of the organization. However, as they have more interactions with the principal or their child's teacher, they may move their trust to one based on the respect or personal regard they are shown or their perceptions of the competence and integrity of the school professionals.

When we enter into repeated exchanges with someone, we typically conduct a give-and-take with them that may be unequal or difficult to measure (Blau, 1986). When we do a favor for someone, we generally expect that it will be returned in the future. When someone does a favor for us, we feel obligated to do something in return in the future. Because we cannot be certain that the future return of favor will occur—or if it does that it will be equally valuable—social exchange involves trust. Once the initial obligation is paid back, further exchanges may happen with more confidence that the person is trustworthy. Therefore, as the number of successful interactions grows, so does the trust.

When a new principal arrives in a school, teachers may be unwilling to immediately begin an instructional reform effort under the new leadership. However, as their social interactions progress and teachers gain some knowledge of the principal, teachers' values, the consistency of their actions, and their sense of responsibility, they may be more willing to enter into more risky interactions. Although their past exchanges have been on smaller projects, their successful completion has allowed trust between the principal and teachers to grow.

SUMMARY

In much of our everyday interactions, we must decide whether or not to place trust in others. When we successfully complete interactions by trusting that others will not cheat us rather than building up complicated monitoring systems, we realize extra benefits from an efficient transaction. Trust becomes even more valuable in places such as schools, where monitoring is not only inefficient but also impossible. Research on trust in schools conceptualized trust as a product of individual perceptions of other people's respect, personal regard, competence, and integrity. But how do we build it? Organizational literature often talks about trust as rooted in single concepts, such as social similarity, contractual obligations, social symbols, or past and future exchanges. This view of trust is static and suggests that trust either exists or does not. It fails to allow for different levels of trust or the growth of trust over time. We need a more complete model of trust building that might make use of these concepts while bringing more depth to the story of how we come to trust one another.

2 Trust Building as a Developmental Process

Although much of organizational behavior theory bases trust on one factor or another, some researchers have developed theories of trust formation as a process. In developing the trust-building process, these theorists use many of the same elements discussed in Chapter 1. However, they order them and use them in combinations to show a progression of behavior that explains the growth of trust rather than merely describing types of trust. This body of work goes beyond the discussion of repeated interactions to map out specific steps in the process that differentiate some social interactions from others.

Lewicki and Bunker (1995) envision a model of trust within work relationships as an evolution that begins with collegial or client-server relations and deterrence-based trust. This form of trust, similar to that produced by contracts, is sustained by the threat of punishment and based on the calculation of what can be gained by cheating versus what can be lost. In this stage, an individual's performance can be evaluated, and successful exchanges are easily recognized. After some successful interactions, the relationship may then move to knowledge-based trust, which is grounded in behavioral predictability. Like trust based on repeated social exchanges, this stage requires regular communication and interaction. If the partnership is successful in its exchanges, the relationship may then move to identification-based trust. This form of trust is based on a full internalization of the other party's desires and intentions. Each party comes to understand what is necessary to sustain the other's trust through the development of a collective identity or the creation of joint goals and shared values.

The Lewicki and Bunker (1995) model of trust is useful in that it proposes that trust evolves over the length of the relationship. This is a vision of trust as a continuum of high trust to low trust rather than a discrete presence or absence of trust. The model also recognizes that trust can operate differently as a relationship deepens, and a relationship can move up and down the continuum if a violation of trust occurs. While useful in an overall conception of a relationship, the Lewicki and Bunker model provides little understanding of what occurs during exchanges that might affect the growth of trust.

Using the context of the business arena, Ring and Van de Ven (1994) propose a model with more detail about cooperative exchanges. In this model, formal structures (laws, arbitration, contracts, etc.) provide the initial boundaries of norms and precedents that define fair dealing. Therefore, the initialization of the relationship is similar to Lewicki and Bunker's (1995) deterrence-based trust. An exchange relationship develops through the repetition of negotiation, commitment, and execution of exchanges. The negotiation stage consists of forming joint expectations about motivations, investments, and perceived uncertainty in the exchange. Like open-ended contracts, feedback during this stage helps to define expectations and intentions. Understanding each other's position increases the likelihood of successful negotiation. The commitment stage consists of the agreement on obligations and rules for the future exchange. Here, roles and rules are formalized into norms of behavior. Common agreement on norms, work roles, and the nature of the work among parties increases the likelihood of establishing formal commitments. The execution stage consists of carrying out the exchange. The outcomes of the execution stage provide information for the next round of negotiations. Ring and Van de Ven suggest that trust grows as a relationship continues to complete successful repetitions of this cycle.

Ring and Van de Ven's (1994) model for cooperation makes an important contribution to theories of trust when considering how organizational roles operate within these exchanges. At the beginning of a relationship, people interact within the parameters of their role. However, as successful exchanges continue, personal ties may overtake the role relationship so that the individuals step beyond formal rules and responsibilities into extra-role behaviors. While this model provides clarity about the processes involved in exchanges, it fails to demonstrate how individuals decide to enter into exchanges and the role that trust plays in making those decisions.

A model by Mayer, Davis, and Schoorman (1995) brings insights into individual decisions to cooperate. In this model, the authors propose that a person will weigh the level of trust in a possible exchange against the level of perceived risk before engaging in an exchange. An individual's level of trust is first dependent on his or her propensity to trust prior to any knowledge of a potential partner. Next, an individual makes an assessment of the trustworthiness of his or her potential partner. Trustworthiness is assessed through perceptions of another's ability, benevolence, and integrity in light of the proposed exchange. The individual must decide whether or not this partner has the ability to complete the exchange. The person also calculates whether or not this partner has good intentions or benevolence toward him or her. Finally, the person assesses the extent to which the partner shares the person's fundamental values. Information gained through the exchange is used to update future perceptions of ability, benevolence, and integrity.

The Mayer, Davis, and Schoorman (1995) model details specific concepts that influence whether or not exchanges take place and whether or not trust advances in the relationship. A key factor from this model is the importance of an individual's propensity to trust. People come with their own base state of trust. Cooperative relationships begin with differing levels of trust based on individual propensities of trust and history of previous interactions between the people in the exchange. As with any setting, members of a school community bring with them a prior history that has shaped their ideas about human motivations in general and their own comfort level in entering situations that involve risk. Some individuals believe that people are basically good and therefore have a higher base propensity to trust. Others have experienced numerous relationship failures, which have made them less open to risk. Therefore, they have a lower propensity to trust in general without regard to the present circumstances.

The concept of an individual's propensity to trust describes the sense of vulnerability that people have in entering trust relationships. The Lewicki and Bunker (1995) model uses a form of deterrence to ease these vulnerabilities in new exchanges. Ring and Van de Ven (1994) also talk of the need for contracts or proxies at the initialization of a relationship. The need to ease vulnerabilities is real for school relationships as well. When a new principal enters a school, teachers often withhold their efforts and enthusiasm until they develop better knowledge of the principal. Therefore, initial exchanges may fall more under the purview of contractual obligations rather than any expanded social construction of teaching. Thus, it is important to note that the behaviors that build trust vary depending on the stage of the relationship.

All three process models emphasize that trust evolves over time through repeated interactions. Although initial exchanges may be governed by contracts or deterrents, knowledge gained from exchanges affects the decision to engage in new exchanges. Mayer, Davis, and Schoorman (1995) bring more information to this part of the process by proposing that individuals weigh the level of risk involved in an exchange against the level of trust they have for their potential partner within the context of the exchange. Therefore, relationships with relatively low trust must engage in low-risk activities. If these activities are successful, then they may enter into increasingly risky exchanges as their level of trust rises with each success.

With the lessons from these process models as a guide, the proposed model of trust building in schools must begin with an easing of the vulnerabilities of the participants to induce them to enter into exchanges. Prior histories may have created a context in which this is quite difficult or relatively easy. Once an initial exchange is established, actors in a school community must enter into repeated interactions so that they gain knowledge of one another's trustworthiness and might attempt increasingly risky exchanges. Like the process models described earlier, this framework for a model of trust building in schools consists of a repetitive process, played out in daily interactions, that progresses from initial interactions that may be based merely on a written contract to a set of interactions based on socially constructed norms.

In applying the Bryk and Schneider (2002) theory of trust in schools to this framework, the social exchanges divide into those that are simply social and promote positive discernments of respect and personal regard and those that are more high risk and promote positive discernments of competence and integrity. Thus, with the inclusion of the base conditions, there are three types of action in trust development: setting the stage for trust, creating opportunities for low-risk interactions, and creating opportunities for more high-risk interactions.

Within this framework, how might the process of trust building be promoted in schools? While mutual dependencies exist across all roles in schools, it is the principal who has the most power in a typical urban school community. A principal holds formal power over the teachers' positions and informal authority over low-income parents who lack an equal education or job status. In this atmosphere, it is incumbent on the principal to reduce the vulnerabilities of others to initiate the growth of trust in the school. The principal is in the best position to bring participants together in low-risk and high-risk exchanges that promote positive discernments of respect, personal regard, competence, and integrity. An examination of the literature on principal leadership and school change provides insights on practices that are linked with successful leadership for school reform. Among these practices are several that could be used to set the stage of the growth of trust, engage participants in low-risk exchanges that are likely to promote mutual respect and personal regard, and create opportunities for high-risk interactions that are likely to promote the exchange of positive discernments of competence and integrity.

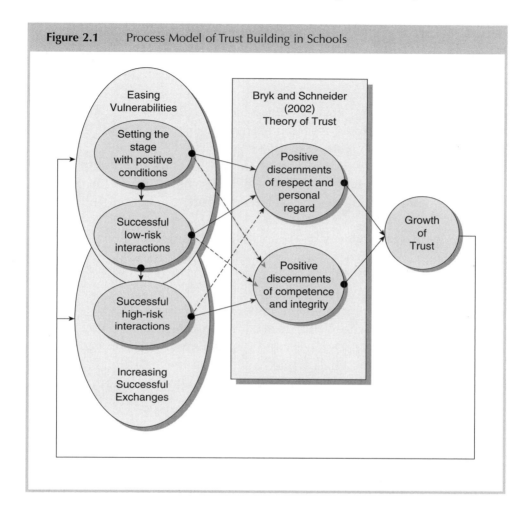

Figure 2.1   Process Model of Trust Building in Schools

SETTING THE STAGE FOR POSITIVE INTERACTIONS

Setting the stage for positive interactions involves putting people in a position where the development of trust is possible. Here the principal might use mechanisms that ease the sense of vulnerability teachers and parents may have so that they will enter into low-risk exchanges. First, the principal may communicate a belief system that puts the needs of the students first as a mechanism for easing others' sense of vulnerability. In doing so, the principal sets the stage for positive interactions in that this is a belief system about which both parents and teachers can easily agree. Second, a principal may need to reshape the faculty to rid a school of oppositional and incompetent faculty members who make positive discernments of respect, competence, and integrity less likely.

Communicating a Vision of Doing What Is Best for Children

When the principal communicates a belief system around doing what is best for children and acts consistently with this belief system, the stage is set for positive interaction in the school, both between principal and teachers and among the teachers (Bryk & Schneider, 2002; Comer & Haynes, 1999). While some organizational research on trust formation calls for leaders to balance their own interests with those of their subordinates, Bryk and Schneider argue that within a school the interests of the children must come first. If teachers believe that decisions are being made for this purpose, they may put aside their own interests and support the work of the principal.

The principal may convey this belief system through symbolic leadership while carrying out daily activities (Bryk, Sebring, Kerbow, Rollow, & Easton, 1998; Deal & Peterson, 1994; Louis & Miles, 1990). The principal's demeanor, use of time, forms of communication, and attention to school ceremonies and rituals are all opportunities to convey his or her vision. A principal must realize that the school culture is communicated in everyday interactions (Deal & Peterson, 1994). Deal and Peterson describe an effective principal who meets several goals while supervising the arrival of children in the morning. In this example, the principal simultaneously performs the following actions:

- Greets students and parents, monitors the bus drivers, and communicates the principal's vision
- Inquires about homework assignments while greeting individual students with a smile and a touch or a hug
- Pays special attention to those who seem unhappy and uses teasing or compliments to engage them with a smile
- Checks in with a school neighbor about whether students have been trampling on his garden while hurrying to school
- Escorts a new student and her parent to the office for paperwork

In short, the principal is conscious of every interaction as an opportunity to both gather information about the school community and transmit his or her vision to its members. These communications serve as reminders of what education should be about—the children.

In essence, principals must take on the role of storyteller when introducing themselves and their style of leadership (Deal & Peterson, 1994; Levitt & March, 1988). Principals must frame organizational actions, routines, and possible reforms with an overall purpose. To further the growth of trust between themselves and teachers and parents the purpose must revolve around doing what is best for the students.

Reshaping the Faculty to Create a Cohesive, Competent Team

As noted in the organizational literature, trust is more easily built between people with similar interests. Thus, setting the stage for trust formation may include reshaping the faculty to bring together teachers with more compatible beliefs. For example, a faculty characterized by racial tensions has major barriers to building trust. Significant individual change would be necessary before trust could be built within the group. Trust is more likely to develop if the principal removes certain key individuals and hires more compatible personalities. In addition, the removal of oppositional personalities helps to rewrite or erase possibly negative organizational histories so that new members are not socialized into the status quo but may move the organization forward by being open to new modes of interacting (Levitt & March, 1988). As such, this theory of trust building involves a selection mechanism where supporters of the principal are brought in as well as cultivated from the existing staff.

In reshaping the faculty, the principal must also remove any teachers who are grossly incompetent (Bryk & Schneider, 2002). Simply put, it is difficult to produce positive discernments of competence and integrity when teachers are not competent and are not acting in the best interests of the children. As noted in the literature, gradations of teacher competence are difficult to judge. However, incompetence in the classroom is more readily noticed. Weak control of the students can be noted by the noise level of the class, frequent referral of students to other classes or the principal's office, and the lack of control of students on trips through the hallways. Incompetent instruction may be discerned as students pass from one grade to another as well as from standardized test results. Incompetent teachers not only harm the children in their classrooms, but they also call into question the dedication and competence of the entire staff. Other teachers and parents not only have difficulty forming trusting relationships with incompetent teachers, but they also question the competence and intentions of the school leadership that allows incompetent teachers to remain. In the end, principals who do not remove incompetent teachers are not acting within the children's best interests.

Some literature on trust in schools identifies supportive leadership as a factor of trust formation. Hoy, Tarter, and Witkoskie (1992) define supportive leadership as friendly, open, and guided by norms of equality. The supportive principal is approachable, helpful, and concerned about the social and professional needs of the staff. The supportive principal motivates the faculty to improve with constructive criticism. In such an atmosphere, teachers feel respected as people and as professionals. They feel safe to voice their needs and concerns with their principal and with one another. Not surprisingly, Hoy et al. found positive relationships between supportive leadership and teacher-principal trust as well as teacher-teacher trust.

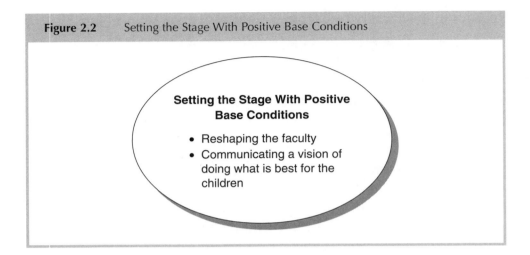

Figure 2.2   Setting the Stage With Positive Base Conditions

Setting the Stage With Positive Base Conditions

- Reshaping the faculty
- Communicating a vision of doing what is best for the children

This type of supportive leadership may work well once trust relationships have been established in a school. Yet when a principal is working to push out teachers who are incompetent or are not committed to improvement, the principal may not necessarily be viewed as a friendly and open person by all of the staff. In the process of removing some faculty, the principal may be providing rewards to those teachers who agree with the principal's vision and creating disincentives to stay to those who do not. Such behavior is not guided by norms of equality. Thus, a principal in the midst of reshaping the faculty does not fit the supportive leadership mold.

Attempts to remove incompetent and oppositional teachers may increase some of the staff's sense of vulnerability in the short term. However, reshaping the faculty eventually decreases anxiety as dissenting and incompetent staff leave and the school's sense of unity grows around a shared vision of schooling. Furthermore, faculty perceptions of the principal's competence and integrity rise if they are able to relate the attempts to reshape the faculty to the principal's dedication to doing what is best for the children.

FOSTERING LOW-RISK EXCHANGES

After setting the stage for positive exchanges, the principal may further ease vulnerabilities by creating opportunities for low-risk interactions that promote the exchange of respect and personal regard. These interactions have the following characteristics:

- They are purely social in nature and often simply involve conversation.
- They may be arranged around easily accomplished projects.

- They come in the form of daily informal social interaction or special school events.

It is important to note that bringing people together does not necessarily result in positive discernments of respect and personal regard. The removal of divisive personalities is an important precursor to successful low-risk exchanges. In addition, as will be discussed later, the principal can set a tone of respect and personal regard that may be used as a model for behavior among teachers and between teachers and parents.

Engaging in Small, Successful Activities as a Forum for Positive Low-Risk Interactions

Bryk et al. (1998) recommend that the principal engage faculty and parents in easily accomplished projects to create a sense of unity and an opportunity for successful social exchange. Painting classrooms, acquiring books for the library, or implementing a new discipline code are all possible activities that may be relatively easy to accomplish and may serve as real indicators that change is underway. Not only is morale improved by the changes, but also participants are given the sense of working together in a successful way. As they interact, they have the opportunity to demonstrate their respect and personal regard for one another in a low-stress arena.

These projects should not only be successful but also arranged in such a way that the participants can recognize their roles in the success. By making the projects meaningful to school improvement yet easily accomplished, participants can put actions to their words and begin to demonstrate their integrity and competence. As with Lewicki and Bunker's (1995) first stage of trust building, early accomplishments and understanding of responsibilities help ease an individual's sense of vulnerability. In this way, early successful projects lay the basis for more high-risk interaction as trust building continues.

Promoting Small-Group Interactions to Ease Vulnerabilities

Opportunities for successful, low-risk exchanges come more easily when meetings are held in a small-group format. Small-group interactions make it easier for participants to engage in meaningful exchanges and achieve consensus (Meier, 1995). In small groups, people are more likely to discuss personal values and goals because individuals feel less vulnerable expressing themselves. Such a process allows a safe and respectful environment for participants to share their perceptions of schooling and their expectations of their roles as teachers. In addition, small groups have an easier time locating commonalities in individual values so that a consensus can be reached in the group (Sergiovanni, 1994). Last, small-group interaction is a setting in which it is easy for like-minded individuals to demonstrate their mutual respect and personal regard.

Small-group interaction is a useful way to begin the change process and bring energy to the activity. Early in the process, small-group interaction works well as a way to gather supporters to begin the work on a project. The energy created by this small group of supporters often motivates others to join the group (Louis & Miles, 1990). Once consensus is achieved within a small group, new ideas can be diffused to the rest of the organization (Levitt & March, 1988).

This smaller-group method holds true for cross-role interaction as well. It is helpful if teachers and parents engage in work on core values and planning separately before being brought into a joint process (Sergiovanni, 1994). Parents and teachers hold unique perspectives on the educational process that may be in conflict. Initial discussions with both groups present confuse the larger areas of disagreement that may fall between the two groups of actors with the smaller, more detailed disagreements that may exist within groups. It is better to come to terms with differences within groups before tackling the larger issues that may exist between groups. In addition, cross-role interaction occurs more smoothly when individuals can address one another from differing groups and represent the entire group's stand on an issue rather than merely their own personal opinion.

While the small-group format is helpful in initiating positive exchanges and may promote the early growth of trust, it may also serve as a barrier to the growth of trust if small groups become exclusionary. New principals often are able to identify supportive individuals on their staff who are eager to work on committees or provide feedback. These individuals are usually the first to be included in small-group activities. Indeed, their open attitudes may provide enthusiasm and energy to early projects. However, the principal must not limit the membership on new committees to these supporters. Rather, the principal should continue to actively recruit other members of the faculty to join in the efforts so that the small-group committee is not seen as an exclusive group of the principal's favorites.

Using Daily Social Interaction to Ease Vulnerabilities

As discussed earlier, principals can use symbolic behavior to communicate their vision (Deal & Peterson, 1994). At the same time, principals are using the daily interactions to demonstrate respect and personal regard for others in the school community. By checking in with a neighbor and escorting a new parent to the office, principals let others see their caring, attentive manner. They communicate to both parents and faculty that individual relationships are important to them and that they treat people accordingly.

Other management tasks along with the morning greeting provide opportunities for positive low-risk interactions. In touring the school several times a day, principals have the opportunity to interact with both teachers and students. Similar to their interactions at the morning greeting, they can ask students about specific lessons, support a teacher as a class passes in the hallway, and answer a question from a school board member they meet along the way. Faculty meetings and parent conferences are additional opportunities to demonstrate respect and personal regard for the parents, teachers, and principal.

Modeling Behavior to Promote Successful Low-Risk Interaction

Effective principals model for the staff the kind of behavior that is appropriate when dealing with each other and, most especially, with parents. While research often notes the importance of principal leadership in setting a tone of high standards, this same principle of leading by example must be used to set a tone for relationships in the school community (Leithwood, 1994; Tschannen-Moran & Hoy, 1998). When teachers are treated like competent professionals who are respected and cared for, they are more likely to treat each other with respect and personal regard.

In addition, principals may act as a buffer between parents and teachers. To build trust, principals may demonstrate the role they envision for parents in their management of daily interactions between teachers and parents. For example, if a parent comes to the principal with a complaint about a teacher's discipline system, and the principal is aware of the teacher's system and believes it is appropriate, the principal must welcome the parent's input and treat him or her with respect. The principal does not need to question the teacher's actions or complain about the parent's interference but must view the problem as a lack of communication between teacher and parent and attempt to bridge the gap by asking the teacher to send a letter home with the students explaining the discipline system. Such interaction reaffirms to the teachers that the parents are to be respected and welcomed into the school. At the same time, the principal models the respect he or she believes is due to the teachers as professionals.

Planning Special Events to Promote Positive Low-Risk Interactions

Special school social events, such as a bowling night for the faculty or holiday potluck dinner for teachers, students, and parents, may also

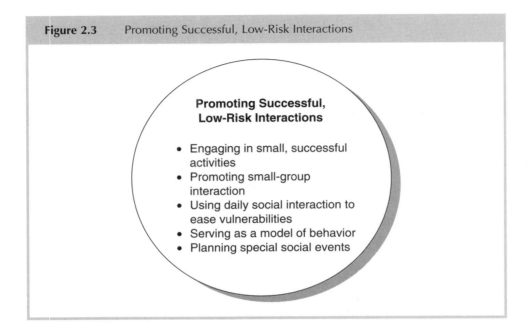

Figure 2.3   Promoting Successful, Low-Risk Interactions

Promoting Successful, Low-Risk Interactions

- Engaging in small, successful activities
- Promoting small-group interaction
- Using daily social interaction to ease vulnerabilities
- Serving as a model of behavior
- Planning special social events

provide opportunities for low-risk exchanges. Bringing people together in fun activities or in times of celebration is an easy way to encourage positive interactions in which they will treat one another with respect and personal regard. A common problem with these activities in low-trust environments is a lack of enthusiasm for attendance. Therefore, a principal may put forward a great personal effort to promote these activities among faculty and parents so that teachers might spend leisure time with each other and with parents. Often, a face-to-face invitation in which a principal communicates that one's attendance is personally important to the principal helps increase attendance. However, this type of one-on-one invitation must remain social rather than implying that there may be career implications if a teacher does not attend. Parent attendance can be promoted by generating schoolwide enthusiasm among the students through signs, announcements, and student help in planning and preparation for the event.

CREATING OPPORTUNITIES FOR HIGH-RISK INTERACTIONS

Once low-risk exchanges are successfully underway, the principal may create more formal structures that provide opportunities for more high-risk exchanges that are likely to promote positive discernments of competency and integrity. These structures are often organized around working together to make the school better. Some possible mechanisms are grade-level meetings; formalized committees; peer evaluation for the faculty; increased shared decision making; and formal and consistent school-home connections, such as newsletters, daily student agendas, and parent seats on committees. Some activities that serve as opportunities for high-risk interactions include developing a school mission around what is best for the children and developing a plan of strategic action around increasing the productivity of the school.

As with low-risk exchanges, the act of bringing people together in high-risk exchanges by itself does not guarantee successful discernments of competence and integrity. First, the stage must have been set by removing incompetent faculty and those who do not put the needs of the children first. In addition, efforts to increase instructional competence of the staff and build a common mission for the school not only serve as formats for high-risk interactions but also make positive discernments more likely.

Implementing Formal Structures of High-Risk Interaction

High-risk interactions that promote positive judgments of competence and integrity come most easily from working together. By creating formal structures to increase these interactions, a principal may promote the growth of trust. For example, teachers often meet together informally to discuss classroom practices. A principal might formalize these interactions by providing time for grade-level meetings on a weekly or bimonthly basis. As teachers organize curriculum and discuss pedagogy, they are more likely to make discernments about the integrity and competence of their colleagues. Similar interactions might be promoted across the school by creating committees to help in policy development and instructional management, such as setting a discipline code or making textbook selections. Peer evaluation among the faculty is a more advanced form of high-risk interaction that can serve as a forum for promoting positive judgments of competence and integrity among the teachers.

The development of consistent, formal home-school connections creates opportunities for discernments of competence and integrity between the school staff and parents. Schools may use monthly newsletters with descriptions of classroom activities as a way to interact with parents. Daily student agendas allow parents to become involved in the curriculum and to make judgments about the teachers' competence. In addition, the requirement of a parent's signature on the agenda gives feedback to the teacher that the parent is supportive of his or her child's education. Finally, creating parent seats on important school committees provides high-risk interactions in which both teacher and parent can make judgments of integrity and competence.

Using the Development of a School
Mission to Promote High-Risk Interactions

Effective-school research has identified a clear school mission as a key input in building positive adult relationships in a school community (Bryk, Lee, & Holland, 1993; Newmann & Associates, 1996). Developing a school mission together is an opportunity for school professionals and parents to publicly express their set of values and map out how they intend to put them into practice in the school. The mission can serve as a guide for the behavior of all adults in the school community. From the mission, faculty may know what is expected of them, and parents may know what to expect the school to accomplish for their children. This is important input for discernments of integrity and competence.

With a clear, articulated goal, teachers are better able to form working teams to achieve specific ends (Elmore, Peterson, & McCarthey, 1996; Grossman, 1992). A stated, clear goal allows individuals to vocalize their own goals by expressing agreement or disagreement with the school mission. In doing so, some teachers discover a shared meaning of their work between themselves and their colleagues. In this way, they can use the discussion about the mission to make positive discernments about each other's integrity. In that a shared goal enables them to improve their own work and the work of the school in general, an articulated mission also helps school participants to make positive discernments about one another's competence.

Sergiovanni (1994) describes this mission creation process as developing a community of mind. Using the ideology of doing what is best for the students as a centering point, the author argues that the principal should hold meetings to determine the core values of the school. He recommends that teachers and parents meet separately at first, then bring the two groups together to compare their visions and combine the two. This combined meeting should be used to clarify and refine the mission.

When significant members of the school community participate in the mission creation process as recommended by Sergiovanni (1994), support for the resulting goals is built into the process. Bryk et al. (1998) describe actively restructuring schools that have principals who reach out to the community to let parents and teachers know that they were part of the process of change and that the school's primary focus was on the care and welfare of the students. This type of cross-role interaction allows groups to address possible conflicts in vision early, with the overarching goal of doing what is best for the students maintaining a bond between individuals and groups.

Pursuing a Strategic Plan of Action
to Further Induce High-Risk Interactions

Another activity that may serve as a vehicle for demonstrations of competence and integrity is the development of a strategic plan of action. Using the mission as a guide, the school staff may develop a plan to determine both long-term planning and day-to-day decision making (Sergiovanni, 1994). This strategic plan may include an agreement on the aims of education, the social significance of student learning, the image of a teacher, and the preferred pedagogy. The process of developing this plan involves the sharing of individual conceptions of teaching and learning and a reflection on educational practices. It reveals individual assumptions about teaching and schooling and allows people to share their expectations of themselves and others in the school community. Such in-depth discussions allow teachers to make judgments of their colleagues' integrity. To the extent that plans are successfully created in these meetings, they also serve as a forum for positive discernments of collegial competence.

Louis and Miles (1990) describe the development of a strategic plan of action as an evolutionary planning process. From their perspective, the principal puts together a coordinating group that represents all stakeholders to outline the plan. Next, the process moves to include all members in the discussion. While the core values of the school remain the same, the strategies used to get there may change over time. In this sense, evolutionary planning is an iterative process. In addition, it is conducted on the level of those who directly use the strategies (i.e., the teachers rather than administrators). The theory suggests that these participants are the ones most in touch with what is or is not needed. The authors note, however, that this type of inclusive planning does not work with groups in conflict. If there is a divided faculty, participatory planning will only increase the hostility among the staff as the sides stick to their positions rather than seeking agreement. This limitation is true in trust building as well. If a faculty is in conflict, such high-risk interactions are not likely to produce positive discernments of integrity or competence.

While it may seem logical to begin the planning process after the core values of the mission have been determined, it is more likely that the discussion about the school mission is also an iterative process that will overlap with developing a strategic plan of action. Discussions on abstract notions such as values lead participants to discuss the implications of these values or the methods of implementing such values. In addition, the agreement on certain values may move the process to the development of a strategic plan, but in debating details of the plan a new discussion of values may surface. Both discussions on values and practices may reveal faculty members who do not agree with the direction the majority of the school is taking or who stand in the way of building a community of professionals. Therefore, while it is best to have a coherent faculty when entering the discussions of values and practices, the processes of planning and reshaping the faculty are likely to occur simultaneously.

Shifting Control From Administrators to Teachers

As argued earlier, good schools operate as networks, and networks are characterized by mutually dependent relationships. Effective management research argues that management's primary role in a network is to create shared-governance partnerships through investment in technical, business, and leadership skills (Miles & Creed, 1995). Eventually, a network organization should have a collegial structure rather than superior-subordinate relationships. This discussion of management theory for networks carries important implications for the organization of schools and the leadership of school principals. As Miles and Creed describe, school principals are indeed dependent on work both upstream in the form of federal, state, and local policy making, and the provision of resources and local authority from the central board. In addition, principals are dependent on the staff in their schools to produce improved instructional quality and greater learning outcomes. This management model, therefore, dictates that principals develop their staff to be continuous learners who share in the school governance.

Shared decision making is often noted in the research on effective principals (Louis & Miles, 1990; Sergiovanni, 1992, 1994). Instructional change is difficult to force on teachers from above. Rather, it is easier to induce teachers to engage with one another in discussions about pedagogy and instructional improvement. Therefore, it makes sense to confer authority over classroom practices to the staff.

Shifting control from the principal to the teachers is both dependent on trust formation and a tool in trust formation. In ceding control, there must already exist some level of trust between principal and teachers. Therefore, shared decision making is a mechanism for trust building that should be used after significant work has been done to ease others' sense of vulnerability through setting the stage to promote low-risk exchanges and to create high-risk interactions. Shared governance offers a forum for trust development in that it requires high-risk interactions that center on improving the work of the school and involves increasing the technical and leadership skills of the teaching staff. In this sense, it promotes positive discernments of others' integrity and competence.

As noted earlier, a principal should not cede significant power until some coherence is built among the faculty. Research in principal leadership has shown that principals need to know when to be directive and assertive and when to back off and allow others to lead change efforts (Louis & Kruse, 1995; Muncey & McQuillan, 1996). Trust formation requires a balance of strong leadership from the principal with a gradual shift in control once the staff members are in place and developed. The key is to cede power to supportive groups while developing further support and talent.

In essence, a principal who wants to build high-trust relationships in a low-trust school might follow Sergiovanni's (1992) evolution from bureaucratic to moral leadership. When the principal enters the school, he or she could use bartering methods to enlist staff cooperation while building a set of core values with the staff and reshaping the faculty appropriately. During this phase, the method of enlisting cooperation changes from a need for reward to a sense of obligation to other people in the school community. Once the principal and faculty are bound together around a set of shared values, people become more self-managing because they are dedicated to doing what is right. This evolution changes the incentive system from an external reward, to an internal reward that comes from working for and with people one cares about, to an intrinsic reward that comes from doing what one believes is morally right. When a school reaches the final stage, the faculty members have formed a collective identity similar to Lewicki and Bunker's (1995) identification-based trust, in which strong relationships survive most violations of trust as long as they do not involve changes to the binding value of doing what is best for the students.

Thus, as the faculty becomes a more coherent whole, the principal can shift more control to them. When within-faculty trust is high, teachers feel more comfortable working together on governance issues. They can disagree with one another without causing divisions in the faculty because they understand that they are all working toward the same goal of doing what is in the best interest of the students. Under this setting, shared decision making is an effective school reform.

ILLUSTRATING A MODEL WITH CASE STUDIES

Reviewing the research gives us a solid foundation from which to develop a model of trust building. However, the model alone lacks the everyday examples that help us visualize these mechanisms in action. To help illuminate the model and demonstrate how it might work within different contexts, the following three chapters present semihistorical case studies

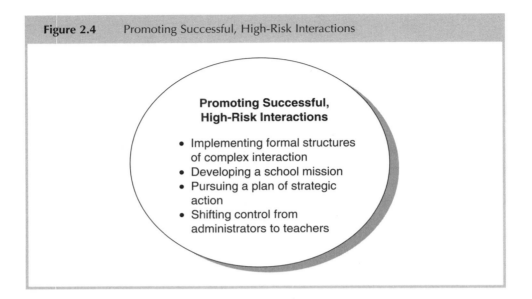

Figure 2.4   Promoting Successful, High-Risk Interactions

Promoting Successful, High-Risk Interactions

- Implementing formal structures of complex interaction
- Developing a school mission
- Pursuing a plan of strategic action
- Shifting control from administrators to teachers

of schools that experienced a growth of trust. The schools were selected using survey and principal personnel data from the Consortium on Chicago School Research (the Consortium). First, a list of schools that experienced a change in leadership just after the Consortium survey in the spring of 1997 was generated. From this list, schools that showed a significant improvement on three Consortium trust measures from 1997 to 1999, as well as improvements in teacher reports of principal leadership, work orientation, and professional community in the 1999 survey, were identified. Of the twenty schools that experienced a change in leadership and participated in the Consortium surveys, four had notable changes in the trust measures, and three of these four agreed to participate in this study on trust building.

The qualitative research in these three schools took place during the 2000–2001 school year. Data were collected through firsthand observations of faculty meetings, local school board meetings, report-card pickups, special school events, and the school improvement planning process. At the end of the observation year, historical interviews were conducted to discern what activities and policy changes were begun after the change in principal leadership and how these changes were perceived by the school community. One-fourth to one-third of the teachers at each school were interviewed in addition to the principal.

During the observations, critical events and behaviors were noted. In addition to gathering a history of what transpired before observations began, the interviews were used to test that others agreed with my assessments of what events were critical to relations in the school and how these events were perceived. Furthermore, the interviews asked about the judgments participants made about their own and others' intentions; the understandings participants had about their own and others' obligations; and the discernments participants made about respect, competence, integrity, and personal regard among the role relationships in the school.

Using the theory of trust building as a guide, the interview and observation data were analyzed to note events and behaviors that relate to developing trust. Specifically, interactions and events that either supported or were antithetical to the key concepts of the trust-building model were noted. For example, in an observation session spent walking a hallway with a principal, her use of the tour to symbolically communicate the mission of the school was noted. In addition, interactions with students, teachers, and parents were recorded. Did the principal demonstrate respect and personal regard? Was she welcoming, warm, and reassuring? School signs, bulletin boards, and decorations were examined for content that communicated a shared vision, expectations of role obligations, or respect and personal regard. From these observations, a case study was developed for each school that gives a historical narrative of trust building.

The cases begin with a description of the school and its surrounding community. Changes in student demographics and standardized test scores in the decade prior to the study are reported, along with a description of the school's previous principal and how the change in leadership from the previous principal to the current one occurred. The cases then discuss the base conditions of trust that the current principal inherited as he or she moved into the position. From there, an accounting of new strategies adopted by the current principal is given, along with the philosophies on leadership and school improvement that the principal gave as reasons for these strategies. Finally, the cases discuss the conditions of trust in the school at the time of the study, how the change in leadership affected changes in interactions within the school, and how these changes fit into the proposed process model of trust building.

The three cases present an interesting array of time points in the trust-building process. The base conditions of trust inherited by these three principals varies from a complete lack of trusting relationships to well-formed relationships that are still improving. The cases begin with a school that experienced very high levels of trust among the adult role relationships. The principal at this school benefited from positive base conditions and was able to identify strategies that would continue to improve relationships and address the few weaknesses that existed to further elevate the levels of trust in the school. Next, a school that had little or no trusting relationships at the time the current principal came into the position is presented. With base conditions at the opposite end of the spectrum from the first case study, this principal relied on an entirely different set of trust-building strategies to move the school into a more positive state of relations. Finally, the third school studied is more moderate in the base state of its trust relationships than the second case study, but not as advanced as the first. This principal inherited a set of relations with some obvious weaknesses that he was able to address using some of the same strategies that both of the other principals used. In doing so, he healed some of the wounds caused by the previous principal. However, he failed to identify the more subtle needs of the teachers and parents to move the trust relationships into new areas of growth.

3 MacNeil Elementary School

Improving a High-Trust School

Located on the northwest side of Chicago, MacNeil Elementary has served an ethnically mixed population over the past fifteen years. Early in the 1990s, its student population was nearly equally divided between White and Hispanic students, with a little over 5% African American and over 10% Asian. During the 1990s, the Hispanic population rose steadily while the others declined so that by the 2000–2001 school year, almost 75% of the student population was Hispanic, less than 20% was White, and the African American and Asian populations hovered near 3% each. This change in the ethnicity of the neighborhood was accompanied by changes in the students' proficiency in English and socioeconomic status. In the early 1990s, less than 20% of the students served had limited English proficiency. This percentage rose to more than 30% by the end of the decade. Even more notable, however, the percentage of low-income students in the school went from less than 60% to more than 80% in those ten years.

Despite these demographic changes, the school produced a steady growth in student achievement as measured by standardized test scores. Whereas in 1990 only 30% of students at MacNeil performed at or above national norms in reading comprehension on the Iowa Tests of Basic Skills (ITBS), by the 2000 school year, 46% of students scored at or above national norms in reading. Similar improvement was seen in mathematics, with scores rising from 36% of students at or above national norms in 1990 to 53% in 2000.

THE PRINCIPAL IN THE OFFICE

At the beginning of this time of change, MacNeil Elementary was led by long-time principal Donald Laslow. A strong authoritarian, Laslow was well liked by both teachers and parents in the school community. He sent a clear message that everyone was to work for the best interests of the children. The goal of the school was set: to improve student learning. As one teacher reported, "With Mr. Laslow, the goal was that the kids were going to behave, they were going to be safe, they were going to do well. 'Do it however you have to do it. Get together and figure out how you have to do it. And if you have any problems, I'm over here.'"

While Laslow made his vision of doing what is best for the students clear, he viewed his role in reaching this goal as that of the administrator. He set school policy. He communicated with the central office. He hired new staff. He addressed parental concerns. In other words, as one teacher noted, "He was the principal in the office."

Teachers were expected to meet administrative deadlines and keep order. Assuming they met these expectations, they were left to decide matters of instruction on their own. A veteran teacher recalls, "[Laslow] was more in charge. He wasn't interested in the details. He wanted the second-grade class to be downstairs at 2:29 exactly. He was an administrator."

Many teachers at MacNeil noted that Laslow was a competent administrator who managed the school well. A primary-grade teacher said, "He was an excellent administrator. He ran the school beautifully. It felt safe." However, as the administrator, Laslow did not view his role as one of building relationships with teachers. One teacher, hired late in Mr. Laslow's tenure, noted, "Mr. Laslow was very detached. He barely said hello to me." So, while many teachers appreciated that their principal provided them with the setting and tools to do their job well, they also found that his clear delineation of roles did not include personal regard or instructional leadership.

For instructional support and collegiality, the teachers at MacNeil turned to one another. Most teachers respected each other. Friendships formed between neighboring classrooms, and there was an overall tone of friendliness in the school that extended throughout the faculty. One teacher who started at MacNeil as a student teacher during this period noted that when she first visited the classrooms of teachers she did not know, she was greeted with the same warmth she experienced later as a colleague and friend of many teachers there.

Despite the friendships and the collaboration to help one another professionally, under Laslow the faculty members at MacNeil functioned independently in their classrooms. Teachers were free to use their own instructional styles as long as the results did not have a noticeably negative impact on their colleagues or on the school. Although friendships sometimes extended between grades, there was little effort to create curricular or instructional coherence across the school. Even within a grade level, teachers often worked together to choose textbooks but then planned how they would use them separately. Thus, students moved from grade to grade in the school experiencing different curricula and a variety of teaching styles.

Just as Laslow did not spend a great deal of time moving throughout the school and interacting with teachers, he was also not especially active with the students. He was not a principal who knew every student's name or kept up with the daily challenges some children and their families met. However, he did make himself available to the parents. Families were welcomed into his office at any time. As part of being the administrator, he accepted the role as liaison between the parents and the school staff. As one teacher noted, parents seemed to respond to his dedication to the interests of their children as well as the efficient operation of the school. "Mr. Laslow was visible. It was different with the parents. He would stop and talk with the parents. . . . The parents loved Mr. Laslow. He ran a tight ship. These were the goals, and these were the goals we were going to get to. I think they appreciated that."

Early in the decade, Laslow hired Dr. Emma Wilson as assistant principal at MacNeil. She provided the necessary counterpart to his administrator role. While he spent most of his day in the office, she moved throughout the school interacting with teachers, students, and parents. She stopped in teachers' rooms to talk about instructional problems. She got to know children and their families. She formed relationships with people. Teachers described her as "caring," "supportive," and "easy to talk to." A veteran teacher noted, "Mr. Laslow wrote letters and responded to letters. [Dr. Wilson] seeks out children to congratulate. She works with kids on math in detention. She's basically a teacher."

When Mr. Laslow announced his retirement at the end of the 1995–1996 school year, Dr. Wilson was high on the list of candidates to replace him. She was recognized by both teachers and parents as well qualified and as a member of their community. Teachers attended local school council (LSC) meetings during the hiring process to voice their support of Dr. Wilson. One parent noted, "Dr. Wilson was definitely highly qualified. The teachers said we were nuts if we didn't use her. She was a known quantity." The LSC agreed with the teachers and hired Dr. Wilson as principal of MacNeil. Because Dr. Wilson had already been with the school for four years, the transition between principals was smooth.

NEW LEADERSHIP: THE PEOPLE'S PRINCIPAL

As principal, Dr. Wilson continued to practice symbolic leadership by using her everyday duties to communicate her vision of schooling. When touring the school several times a day, she stopped in classrooms to observe instruction, check on new or substitute teachers, or attend important classroom events. She also used these tours as opportunities to greet children, parents, and teachers in the hallways, calling them by name and often asking them about people or events that were important to them. On one such tour, Dr. Wilson was observed asking one child if he was feeling better after being absent the day before and asking another child if he did better on his most recent math test. Such comments conveyed to the children that they were important, that people at the school cared for them and missed them when they were not there, and that people at the school cared that they were learning.

Dr. Wilson expanded on these interactions during her daily routines of greeting children in front of the school in the morning and seeing them off in the afternoon. In all kinds of weather, she stood on the sidewalk by the front doors talking with parents and children. Some encounters with parents involved a brief hello or wave. With others, she asked about other family members or how their jobs were going. At times, she talked with parents about their child's work in the classroom or behavior in the school. One teacher reported that Dr. Wilson "[made] a point of knowing something about each of the families." In this way, Dr. Wilson used her daily routines to make parents feel comfortable in the school and to communicate with them that the school cares about them and their children.

Following Dr. Wilson's lead, many teachers at MacNeil began to make themselves available to the children and their parents by greeting them outside the school in the morning and seeing them off again in the afternoon. A first-year teacher at the school talked about how the principal set the pattern for him: "She goes out of her way to build relationships with parents. She's out front every day greeting kids and parents. . . . I go outside after school to meet with parents as well." By standing out front before and after school, both teachers and the principal greatly increased their opportunities for positive interactions with the students and parents. In addition, they communicated to the parents that they wanted to develop relationships with them and that the children were important to the teachers. As one teacher noted, "When you go to pick up your students outside [in the morning], there's a lot of parents. So I think that encourages parents to interact with us a little more."

With a vision of schooling that centered on building relationships and a school mission that included "provid[ing] a well-rounded quality educational experience for the community," Dr. Wilson brought a program called the Responsive Classroom to MacNeil. Although she noted that they were "constantly refining the mission, taking time to reflect on practices and to verbalize it," she believed that the program was key to putting the mission into practice. Developed by classroom teachers, Responsive Classroom is an approach to teaching and learning that emphasizes the social interactions surrounding learning as well as the academic curriculum. The program promotes teaching children social skills such as cooperation, empathy, responsibility, assertion, and self-control so that they can achieve more academically. It stresses the importance of building relationships with parents, students, and fellow teachers as part of creating a learning environment for children.

Dr. Wilson used Responsive Classroom as a model for how she treated her faculty as well. "The teachers are an extended family. . . . I use the Responsive Classroom principles with the faculty. These are adult learners. In a sense, the teacher-student relationship extends to us with the principal as teacher." When comparing her style of leadership with Mr. Laslow's, she noted, "There has been a change in principal-teacher relations [since I became principal]. It looks more open. We feel support from one another. They know they can say things to me. I began by doing little things like writing personal notes to them. I pop into classes. I know the kids." The teachers agreed that Dr. Wilson provided supportive guidance as they continued their efforts to improve. One teacher talked of the principal's respectful way of addressing problem areas. "She's very interested in us as people as well as teachers. . . . And when there's an issue that needs to be dealt with, she'll address it very positively, saying, 'This is something we need to work on.' Nothing negative. Nothing threatening. . . . [She'll say,] 'Hey I understand it gets difficult. Let's work on it.'" While Dr. Wilson said that "competency is not an issue" at MacNeil, she also noted that the faculty still had a dissenting member. "I gave people the opportunity to blend. I have one teacher who is an 8 to 2:30 person without connections, isolated. I expect that person to leave soon."

One of Dr. Wilson's top goals as principal was to improve instruction at MacNeil. Her plan was to increase "grade-level collaboration and provide more technical support." As a senior teacher reported, this goal was made clear to the faculty: "She has stronger ideas about the educational process [than the former principal]. She wants everyone on the same track." To increase teacher competence, she introduced numerous programs on instructional methods and curricular content. Like Responsive Classroom, many of these programs targeted the entire school. During the first few years of her administration, the school adopted the Accelerated Reader program, a schoolwide math program with monthly inservice training, and a technology infusion program. These programs provided continuous training and feedback sessions for the entire faculty for at least the first year of implementation.

Dr. Wilson used these efforts to improve instruction as central activities for increasing collaboration among the staff, another of her key goals. She placed teachers who already worked together informally on committees to assess the proposed instructional programs. A primary-grade teacher reported, "She went to the committees for many decisions. . . . Some of the bigger programs, the entire faculty voted on." She also instituted more formal arrangements for grade-level meetings and rearranged class scheduling to create time during the school day for these meetings. Over time, more decisions were delegated to committees. Grade-level committees chose their own reading programs. Committees led the planning for special school events, such as a multicultural fair and a parent open house. Although more decision-making power was slowly distributed to committees, as one teacher noted, Dr. Wilson still provided her guidance and support so that the committees could accomplish their new duties: "She'll give you responsibility, yet help you succeed with that responsibility."

Teacher-led committees were even responsible for important school governance activities, such as drafting the annual school improvement plan (SIP). The SIP is an annual report required by the central office that evaluates how the school is doing in key areas and details which efforts will be made to improve in those areas during the following academic year. When done well, it serves as the school's strategic plan of action. At MacNeil, the process of developing this plan was led by a voluntary committee of teachers with open participation. The team of teachers held two evening planning sessions from 5:00 P.M. to 8:00 P.M., during which the teachers invited parents to actively participate. One session was held at the beginning of the process, and interested parents were asked to formally join the committee if possible. The second session was held later in the process so that parents could voice their opinions before the final report was drafted. In addition to open sessions, forms were sent home to parents and teachers asking them for written input, even if they were unable to attend meetings or join the committee. Throughout the process, the assistant principal took on administrative tasks, such as organizing meetings and typing drafts of the SIP. However, the teacher-led committee, along with a few parents, was the author of the document.

Moving decisions to teacher committees was part of Dr. Wilson's plan to change the school's understanding of leadership and institute a shared governance plan. In her words, "This is not the job of one person. It takes a whole community. . . . If you have a voice, then you take a role." Recognizing the necessity of sharing leadership with the faculty and parents, Dr. Wilson noted, "You have to be working in concert." To further this, she used faculty members to conduct an internal review of the school. A number of teachers, some volunteers and some picked by the principal, received training offered by the central office. They then conducted observations of their colleagues' teaching to make an overall assessment of whether or not the school was meeting its instructional goals. The results of this process served as the base from which to work on planning for the next school year. Most teachers found the observations so helpful that they asked Dr. Wilson for the opportunity to have more observations of the classrooms in grades immediately above and below their own level.

Early in her administration, Dr. Wilson identified a need to create more opportunities for parent and community involvement in the school. As she put it, "The parents aren't as much a partner as we would like. There's a lot of parent involvement in the primary grades, but it fades as kids get older." She began to address the problem by opening doors for parents experiencing a language barrier with the school. Using some of the increased federal funding that accompanied the increase in low-income children, she began English instruction for parents at the school. This program was so successful that one graduate became a teacher's aide for the kindergarten class, and another took a position in the office. Then, she instituted schoolwide activities to draw parents to the schools such as a family reading night; a math, science, and technology night; school softball teams for the upper grades; and a community garden. Many of the activities surpassed expectations, such as the family reading night, which had more than 300 people attending. In addition, to accommodate the work schedules of the parents at MacNeil, the school extended the time allotted for report card pickup until 7:00 P.M.

Beyond efforts aimed at bringing parents into the school, Dr. Wilson also created new formats for communicating with the parents and letting them know what they could do to help their child succeed in school. First, she proposed that each student take home a daily agenda, which outlined for the parents all homework assignments and encouraged parents to work with their children on certain activities. Parents were required to sign the agendas each day. At a minimum, school personnel hoped that the agendas gave parents the opportunity to talk with their children about their schoolwork.

Second, Dr. Wilson used a monthly newsletter to inform parents about the work of the school. She wrote a general message about school activities, inviting parent participation in special events, such as open houses, and special committees, such as the one formed to write the annual SIP. In addition, on a rotating basis, she asked teachers to write a summary of the curriculum and activities of each classroom. In these summaries, teachers talked about working on a unit on money in math and locating summer vacation spots on the map in geography. They also noted recent field trips and how they fit into the curriculum.

In this newsletter, parents could find dates and locations of important meetings or student performances. In addition, the messages from Dr. Wilson and the teachers made clear the ways in which parents could partner with the school in educating their children. Dr. Wilson wrote to parents, "Help support our educational program by attending PTA meetings, checking student agendas daily for homework, and volunteering. Successful schools are a combined effort of dedicated teachers, involved parents, and an active community" (newsletter from April 2001). Each month's message ended with a similar request.

Finally, Dr. Wilson created a school-community representative position to help generate parent participation in the classroom. The person in this role, filled by a Spanish-speaking parent, attended PTA meetings and networked with parents in the neighborhood to both represent their interests and encourage their participation. In doing so, she committed valuable school resources to create a formal parental role in the school.

Beyond parent participation, Dr. Wilson recognized that the surrounding community had many resources of which the school could make use. She solicited and promoted programs to bring in tutors and mentors from area businesses. An office supply company sent employees to tutor students one day a week. A sports organization supplied employees to mentor students after school. In both cases, Dr. Wilson asked the teachers to help identify students most in need of educational or emotional support. In addition, she asked for grants from neighboring businesses to supply student incentives or support specific improvement projects. Finally, Dr. Wilson remained open to possible benefits to the school from university studies or programs provided by nonprofit agencies. She welcomed the local YMCA to propose an afterschool program to the local school board. She also asked researchers to present their proposal for an asthma study to the board. A committee was formed to evaluate the YMCA proposal, and the asthma study was unanimously accepted because it would provide enormous medical benefits to the students and their families.

REFINING RELATIONSHIPS
FOR HIGHER LEVELS OF TRUST

When Dr. Wilson became principal at MacNeil, she inherited a set of relationships that were already functioning with high levels of trust. The parents in the neighborhood recognized the school's dedication to the children. The teachers were cooperative, and many were friends. Most of the faculty viewed Mr. Laslow, the previous principal, as a competent manager who had acted with integrity and treated them with respect.

Even with this positive base state of relations, there were some vulnerabilities in the relationships formed under the previous principal. First, Laslow's relationship with the faculty lacked the element of personal regard. Teachers were not friends with Mr. Laslow. In general, he did not spend his time ensuring that they were happy, either personally or professionally. Most teachers did not feel that he cared for them beyond whether or not they were doing their jobs.

Second, while some teachers were friends with one another, teachers did not have strong trust among them that was based on professional relationships. There was a general feeling of respect throughout the faculty, and many teachers had a high mutual personal regard. There were no signs of incompetence. However, teachers did not have many opportunities to actually work together and thereby demonstrate their integrity and competence to each other. Thus, their interactions remained simply social.

Finally, the relationship between the parents and the school personnel was one of deference to authority under Laslow. As long as Mr. Laslow continued to manage an efficient operation at the school, parents left the details of their child's education to the teachers and school administrators. The school professionals were respectful with the parents. The parents perceived them to be competent and to work for the best interests of the children. However, there was not a lot of interaction to support these perceptions. For the most part, parents trusted the school because they had not seen anything to breed mistrust.

In some ways, the entrance of Dr. Wilson as the assistant principal alleviated part of the vulnerability in these relationships. Dr. Wilson formed caring friendships with the teachers. She interacted with them on a daily basis, inquiring about their health, interests, or family matters. In addition, she supported them professionally by talking with them about matters of instruction and discipline. Dr. Wilson formed similar relationships with the students and their families. She not only knew students' names, but she also knew their siblings and their parents. She would ask them about a recent test or homework problem. She noticed if they were absent and asked how they were doing the next time she saw them in school. In short, she had numerous interactions with teachers, students, and parents in which she could convey not only respect, competence, and integrity but also the personal regard she held for them. The effect of these interactions was only strengthened when Dr. Wilson became principal at MacNeil.

As a newcomer to MacNeil, Dr. Wilson put the faculty and the parents at ease by articulating a vision they could embrace—one that put the children first. In communicating her vision, Dr. Wilson was also engaged in low-risk interactions that would promote positive discernments of respect and personal regard. Her use of symbolic leadership involved interactions that communicated respect. By inquiring about family life at home with parents, she not only communicated a vision that put the interests of children first but also one that showed that she had personal regard for the family. The use of Responsive Classroom as a key component in accomplishing the school mission also promoted mutual respect and personal regard among teachers and students. In fact, this program set the tone for relationships between the principal and teachers as well as among teachers.

Using the small-group interaction that already existed among the teachers, she created more formal opportunities for teachers to interact. In addition, she set the tasks of increasing instructional competence and coherence as the goals around which they should interact. Teachers were given the opportunity to help develop a plan of strategic action to reach these goals. Over time, decision making was increasingly shared with teacher committees.

The interactions among teachers on these committees helped them to continue to develop relationships based on mutual respect and personal regard. One teacher reported, "We get along extremely well. We have a lot of fun together." In addition, teachers were able to gain firsthand knowledge about their colleagues' competence and integrity by listening to them talk about instruction and their dedication to teaching in the meetings and also by observing them putting their beliefs and skills into action in the classroom. In arguing for the adoption of a certain textbook or instructional method, a teacher would have to demonstrate why the textbook or instructional method was best for the children. A primary-grade teacher talked about how their mutual trust made these discussions more productive. "Even with personality conflicts, there's an understanding that there's a goal that everyone has to meet. They can work through it. . . . I think the respect we have for one another is based on putting yourself in someone else's place." The schoolwide curriculum changes created additional opportunities to promote positive perceptions of competence and integrity, not only by increasing individuals' competence but also by providing inservice training sessions in which professional discussions were modeled and fostered.

Dr. Wilson's model for interacting with parents before and after school gave teachers and parents the opportunity to form personal bonds with one another. In daily greetings, they were able to demonstrate their mutual respect. As teachers showed care and concern for the students and their families, some of these bonds expanded to include an element of personal regard. Teachers became familiar with their students' parents and siblings from these daily visits. They were able to use this knowledge to inquire about how the family's day was going and what new things had happened. In addition, they could comment on what had happened with the student that day that the parent might find interesting. Such exchanges could convey the teacher's respect and regard for the family.

The new, formal opportunities for parent involvement instituted by Dr. Wilson increased the interaction between teachers and parents around matters of education. Parents knew more about the work of the school through the newsletter, family nights, and daily agendas. Through this information, they were able to make better assessments of the teachers' competence and integrity. In addition, parents were asked to take part in the work of the school by monitoring homework using the agendas, reading with their children at home, and joining committees that decided important governance matters in the school. Through these formalized structures, teachers were given more accurate feedback on the competence and integrity of the parents.

The increased trust between teachers and parents was illustrated at a faculty meeting in which teachers were presented with the latest initiative from the central office. In an effort to balance some of the high stakes that schools, teachers, and students were experiencing during an administration focused on raising standardized test scores, the central office designed a "parent report card," which teachers and school administrators were expected to use to grade parents on their performance in their child's education. Parents would be assessed on having their child at school each day—on time, prepared for the school day, and with homework completed. When teachers at MacNeil were shown the report card, many spoke about how offensive it was to parents. One teacher said, "How can they grade parents on things like this? The parents are doing their best for the kids. When both parents are working, how can you grade them on whether or not their child was picked up on time?" Rather than taking an opportunity to evaluate parents as the teachers themselves were being evaluated by the system, the faculty at MacNeil defended the parents' motivations and intentions. In the end, the teachers and administrators at MacNeil refused to send out the parent report cards.

SUMMARY

Five years into Dr. Wilson's tenure as principal, Consortium measures of trust across all adult role relationships increased notably. Teacher-parent trust was rising throughout the Chicago public school system, and MacNeil remained well above the average measure of trust and far surpassed the level of trust in other schools serving similar students. Teacher-teacher trust at MacNeil continued to grow throughout Dr. Wilson's tenure and continued to be above average for the system and for schools serving similar students. Finally, teacher-principal trust soared from slightly above average in 1994 to that of one of the top schools in the system by 1999.

As predicted by the literature on trust in organizations, the base conditions of trust are an important consideration when examining how trust is built in schools. Principals who enter a new school where trust levels are relatively high between teachers and parents and among the teachers themselves may need to put forth some effort to set the stage for trust between themselves, the teachers, and the parents and engage early in low-risk interactions. However, if successful in low-risk interactions, these schools can move rather quickly into high-risk activities.

Dr. Wilson was able to articulate her vision of schooling and engage in positive daily interactions with the faculty and parents at MacNeil during her tenure as assistant principal. Teacher-teacher and teacher-parent trust were relatively high when she became principal. Therefore, she invested most of her efforts as principal to increasing high-risk interactions to further build trust. While still promoting lower-risk social interactions, Dr. Wilson established committees of teachers and parents, structured the school day to increase meeting time, and put real decision-making power into the hands of these committees. The interaction between members on these committees helped them to continue to develop relationships based on mutual respect and personal regard. In addition, teachers and parents on the committees were able to gain firsthand knowledge about their colleagues' competence and integrity by listening to them talk about matters of instruction, their dedication to the school, and their own beliefs about education. In sum, Dr. Wilson inherited a well-functioning set of relationships that she helped grow into a school that was characterized by trust.

4 Mills Elementary School

Starting From a Lack of Trust

L ike MacNeil, the community served by Mills Elementary experienced dramatic demographic changes from 1990 to 2000. Located on the near southwest side of Chicago, the school sits in a neighborhood that at one time was mostly made up of White, blue-collar families. By the beginning of the 1990s, however, a sizable Hispanic population had moved into the community, and the racial composition of the school's student body was nearly 53% Hispanic, 38% White, and 8% Black. As the community diversified, many White families fled to other areas of the city or suburbs. Many other families that chose to stay in the neighborhood moved their children to private schools so that eventually the number of White students in the school underrepresented the number of White families still living in the community. Overall, the racial composition changes in the neighborhood were not well accepted by many of the White families who remained.

As the city adopted local control of schools early in the 1990s, Mills became a prime battlefield over which White families fought to retain control in the neighborhood. A motivated, organized, and relatively well-educated group, these families were able to quickly take advantage of the new process of electing a local school board for Mills. As a result, all parent and community representative positions on the new local school council were filled by White men and women who were opposed to the minority immigration in the community.

Despite efforts to stem the changes, the neighborhood continued to evolve over the decade so that by the year 2000 Mills served a student population consisting of 80% Hispanic, 17% White, 2% Black, and 4% Asian students. The strong upswing in Hispanics also brought a change in English proficiency from 10% of the students being limited-English proficient in 1991 to 24% in 2000. However, there was little change in the percentage of students coming from low-income families, which remained near 94% in 2000.

While the racial tensions of the community spilled over into Mills, the school was able to raise test scores in both reading and mathematics over the same time period. At the beginning of the decade, 23% of the students scored at or above national norms on the ITBS in reading, and 36% of students met the standard in math. By the end of the decade, 33% of the students were at or above national norms in reading, and nearly 59% were at or above national norms in math. Thus, the school experienced a growth in productivity despite the tensions surrounding it.

A SCHOOL IN CONFLICT

In the early 1990s, Mills Elementary was led by Principal William Simmons, a veteran administrator who had been in the position for decades. As a group of White parents and community members came together to fight the perceived threat from the influx of Hispanic families in the community, they recruited Simmons as their ally. They viewed the school as a key battleground in their war on change. Their main goal was to prevent the school from adopting a bilingual program. At the beginning of the 1990s, neither Simmons nor the existing staff at Mills was qualified to run a bilingual program. Thus, the principal willingly accepted the support of this group of parents.

The faculty at Mills was also marked by racial tension. With changes in the city population overall, the pool of teaching candidates in Chicago became filled increasingly by minorities. As a result, teaching vacancies at Mills were sometimes filled by people of African American or Hispanic descent. These newcomers were not welcomed by many of their senior, White colleagues. As one of these teachers stated, "[M]inorities were not wanted in the school. . . . There was a racial divide among the faculty. It was really bad. I mean, really bad."

Mr. Simmons did little to ease the racial divide in the faculty. Rather, he depended on some of his senior teachers to provide him with feedback and help in governance. A Black teacher noted, "[Mr. Simmons] had a clique. They ran the school with a core group of parents." Some teachers saw this dependence on senior staff as part of the principal's lack of governance. One teacher noted, "[He] didn't do much. He stayed in his office."

Some of his inaction and dependence on others might be explained by Mr. Simmons's growing health problems. Early in the decade, the staff at Mills became aware that their principal was fighting cancer. The illness and its treatment became so bad that he had to abruptly retire in 1994. The central office of the school board took this opportunity to appoint an interim principal who more closely matched the cultural and racial background of the majority of the students at Mills. They chose Carmen Munez, a Latina who had a prominent position at the central office and was a strong proponent of bilingual education.

The transition from Mr. Simmons to Mrs. Munez was marked by controversy. The local school council (LSC), consisting entirely of White parents and community members, protested the board's appointment. Mrs. Munez recalls, "They wanted one of the teachers here to be appointed principal. They wanted a new White male." The LSC organized parents and community members to formally rally, which gained the attention of local newspapers and television news reports. The central office stood firm in its support of Mrs. Munez. With her appointment as interim principal, she had three years before the LSC had formal power to replace her.

A PRINCIPAL UNDER SIEGE

Mills offered many challenges for its new principal. Many teachers were openly hostile with each other and with Mrs. Munez. The parents who were active in school governance were also opposed to her appointment. This group controlled much of her fate in that they could veto changes in school policy that required discretionary funding, and in three years they would vote to renew or release her contract.

Mrs. Munez recognized that this volatile situation required both a great deal of diplomacy and a strong hand of leadership. Her first priority was to build relationships between herself and her staff members. She began by taking those she identified as key players out to dinner. Away from the school, one on one, she asked these individuals about their philosophies of teaching and the direction they thought the school should go. She conveyed her own beliefs about education and let them know that Mills would be a school dedicated to the needs of its students. She told them that this would be the basis of her leadership.

She also immediately instituted policy changes that came from those meetings. For example, she took teachers off lunchroom duty and instituted meetings for the nonfaculty school staff members to keep them informed of school matters. She called these changes "easy wins" because they cost her relatively little in terms of time and money but meant a great deal to teachers and staff.

At the beginning of the next school year, she met with staff members individually to thank them for the work they had been doing in the school. She used these meetings to get their feedback on the school policy and her leadership. In addition, she let them know what she thought were their strengths and in what areas she thought they could improve. During this same time, she took the faculty to a team-building seminar conducted by a local university. There, they engaged in exercises that were designed to promote communication and positive social interaction.

In everyday interactions, Mrs. Munez reinforced her intentions to put the needs of the children first. She often openly said, "We are here for the children. They are our first priority." She was often observed interacting with children in the hallways, sometimes stepping in to regain order among an unruly group of students, other times playfully reminding students to work harder on their homework. She also used classroom assignments, project funding, and supplies as rewards for teachers who adopted the instructional techniques she endorsed. Even with small programs, such as instituting parent safety patrols, funding prizes for the highest achieving students, and providing nutrition classes for parents, Mrs. Munez kept her focus on all of her students' needs.

Mrs. Munez openly communicated her expectations with her staff. One teacher noted that the principal was very vocal in her support of activity centers in the early grades. This teacher had never used centers but was compelled to change her teaching strategy to include them when it meant extra resources for her classroom. In the end, the teacher appreciated both the changes activity centers brought to her classroom and Mrs. Munez's consistency in following through with the resources.

Despite these attempts to promote more positive relationships between herself and the staff and among the faculty members, from the beginning it was clear to Mrs. Munez that some individuals were not open to change. As one teacher noted, some on the faculty were unhappy with her appointment and moved to other schools: "Teachers left who didn't support her." Others were encouraged to leave when they lost status and resources as their colleagues were rewarded for more positive behavior. "She pushed staff to retire. Those that left were older, resentful, more negative about minorities." Some teachers, however, were simply asked to leave. Mrs. Munez recalls repeatedly telling one teacher that she was not working in the best interests of the children and that she needed to improve. After some time when the teacher showed no efforts to improve, the principal asked her to look for another teaching position. "I told her," Mrs. Munez recalls, "she did not belong at Mills." Incredibly, Mrs. Munez replaced twenty-one of twenty-six faculty members during the first five years of her tenure.

Mrs. Munez's second major effort involved developing a support base among the parents. Because her student population was majority Hispanic, she concentrated on mobilizing a group of Hispanic parents, rather than trying to win the support of the hostile parent group that controlled the local school board. She hired a bilingual staff assistant to work in the school office, so parents could communicate with staff on basic school matters. Whenever possible, she filled vacant faculty and staff positions with Spanish speakers.

While Mrs. Munez sought to move the school to better serve its Hispanic population, she also tried to educate the parents on how they could assist in the work of the school. She formed several parent committees, such as a bilingual committee, and actively recruited parents to participate. She organized a parent group that met regularly at the school for socializing and informational lectures. Most important, she identified parents with leadership potential and encouraged them to run for the local school board. With willing candidates identified, Mrs. Munez was able to use the parent committees and social parent group as informal vehicles for their campaigns. The Hispanic parents were mobilized not only for the work of the school but also to transform the principal's support on the LSC. This not only helped Mrs. Munez gain funding for her policy changes but also helped to ensure her future as the principal.

By the beginning of the 2000–2001 academic year, only two members of the original LSC remained on the council. One of these members had been reelected as community representative but did not live within the school zone. Mrs. Munez protested her election with the central office and was successful in having her removed from the LSC. However, the local city councilman's office used political connections to have the LSC member reinstated. After her reinstatement, this LSC member, along with the other remaining original member, was absent from the scheduled LSC meetings. Therefore, Mrs. Munez organized a vote of the LSC to remove the missing members, which was unanimously passed by the council.

Overall, Mrs. Munez used strong leadership to enact change among both faculty and parents. At the end of her first five years at Mills, over 80% of the faculty had been replaced, and the local school board was entirely made up of Hispanic parents and community members, with one Hispanic teacher representative and one Black teacher representative. However, the strong leadership that was required early on had not yet given way to sharing power with teachers and parents. There were no formal structures such as committees for teachers to help shape school policy. Faculty meetings usually consisted of Mrs. Munez informing teachers of new business and were rarely interactive. The parent committees and local school board were staffed by parents that were entirely supportive of Mrs. Munez. The hostile atmosphere of LSC meetings had been replaced with an uncritical calm. A parent from each of the parent committees reported on the month's events, Mrs. Munez reported on any changes in spending, and few questions were raised from either board members or parents from the committees.

Although the principal did inform the board on changes in the faculty or their placement, matters of instruction were not discussed.

Even the board's vote on the school's improvement plan appeared to be perfunctory. This annual report, required by the central office, lays out in detail which programs and policies the school plans to implement to reach its stated goals. At many schools, there is heated discussion about not only what programs and policies are chosen and where funding is allocated but also what the actual goals of the school are. At Mills, the plan was drawn up by Mrs. Munez and one other staff member. They asked for and incorporated some written suggestions from teachers and staff. However, copies of the plan were not distributed to the board before they were to vote on its approval. Rather, to save on copying costs, a copy was made available for reading at the school's office. On the night of the vote, Mrs. Munez gave a ten-minute summary of the plan, which was limited to a detailed recitation of the budget from the prior year and what the dollar figures were projected to be under the new plan for the upcoming year. There was no explanation for the budget changes or the programs behind the numbers. The board members listened quietly and voted unanimously to approve the new plan.

DEVELOPING RELATIONSHIPS FROM THE LOWEST LEVELS OF TRUST

Mrs. Munez began her tenure at Mills with relationships that were characterized by a lack of trust. Caught in the middle of a community's racial tensions, the school's focus had turned to race as well. This struggle permeated all role relationships at Mills.

As noted earlier, the Mills faculty was marked by divisions similar to the community as a whole. Minority teachers felt outcast by their White colleagues. Not only were the more senior staff unfriendly to the minority newcomers, but they also often refused to treat them with basic levels of respect: Greetings were not exchanged at the time clock in the morning; smiles were not offered when passing in the hallway. In such an atmosphere, many relationships characterized by personal regard were out of the question. In addition, judgments of competence and integrity were negatively influenced by perceptions of race and prejudice.

The principal-teacher relationship had many of the same problems. Under the old leadership, the status of the relationship depended on the teacher's race. White teachers, mostly senior staff, were quite friendly with Mr. Simmons. However, minority teachers felt that they had no voice with the principal. They viewed his style as playing favorites at best and acting with racial prejudice at worst. As such, even if the principal was cordial with them, there was no perception of personal regard. And since Mr. Simmons was not addressing the needs of his majority Hispanic student body, minority teachers could not make positive discernments of his competence or integrity.

Mrs. Munez stepped into the role of principal with less favorable conditions for trust with the teachers than what Mr. Simmons had when he left. The White, senior staff members who supported the former principal were openly in opposition to the appointment of Mrs. Munez. At the same time, many of the minority teachers were not open to trusting anyone put in the position. Rather, they cautiously took a wait-and-see approach. The new principal would have to earn every aspect of their trust.

Relationships between the principal and the parents and between the teachers and parents mirrored that of the principal and teachers. That is, the state of the relationship often depended on the race of the participants. In general, White parents felt respected by the principal and teachers. Many of them were active in the school and its governance. They felt that the school was acting in the best interests of their children, so they held positive views of the school staff members' competence and integrity.

Minority parents experienced a different school. As a group, the Hispanic parents were not politically organized or active. Many of them treated the school with deference, leaving the education of their children to the professionals. The school, in turn, did not reach out to the Hispanic parents. As one teacher noted, "Before, bilingual parents were not welcome. There was no translator." In many cases, the Hispanic parents simply could not communicate with the principal or teachers at Mills even if they tried.

The Mills case study demonstrates how the trust-building model functions differently for schools that start with a low base state of trust. From the time of her arrival at Mills, Mrs. Munez implemented changes that would set the stage for the growth of trust. She began by articulating a vision that put the needs of the children first and then reshaped the faculty to remove teachers who were incompetent or had divisive personalities. Next, Mrs. Munez created opportunities for low-risk interactions between herself and the teachers and parents.

Teachers initially responded positively to her message. One of the teachers hired by Mrs. Munez talked about her impressions of the school's leadership: "Everything possible is being done to improve student learning . . . I like [Mrs. Munez]. She has a tough job. She rewards those who are doing well." Another teacher who had been at the school through the transition also talked favorably of Mrs. Munez: "She's a good leader. She has a good vision."

By pushing out some faculty members, Mrs. Munez successfully eliminated racial tensions among the staff members. In doing so, she restored basic respect and personal regard in teacher relations. One teacher reported that faculty members at Mills were "social with one another." Another teacher who had been on the staff through the transition noted, "Things are more comfortable now. People get along. There is camaraderie. Teachers talk to each other."

While these efforts were successful in initiating trusting relationships, Mrs. Munez did not continue to build trust by promoting more high-risk interactions. She did not form teacher committees or encourage teachers to work with one another on school improvement efforts. She maintained a strong, centralized leadership style with all decision making for the school under her authority. This lack of shared power with the faculty concerned the teachers. Many teachers felt that Mrs. Munez did not consult with them even in an advisory capacity when making decisions, let alone delegate any real authority to them. A veteran teacher talked about how this lack of discussion about policy put the teachers in a difficult position. "She makes the decisions. The faculty must tell her when they disagree."

The absence of consultation and shared decision making was especially problematic given the amount of staff turnover. When teachers were removed due to clear problems, such as prejudice or incompetence, other faculty members were supportive. However, as time went on and the changes in the staff continued, teachers began to feel a little more vulnerable and less able to speak their minds. A veteran teacher explained that no one wanted to openly disagree with the principal: "Teachers were backing her contract renewal. Now there are mixed feelings, some anxiety. There's a lack of communication. . . . I tell her [when I disagree]. Others are scared. There's a fear of retribution." A newer teacher also talked of how the continued teacher turnover reflected negatively on the principal's leadership. "The staff needs to stabilize. . . . She keeps us all on our toes. There's no finger on what she'll do or not do."

In the end, Mrs. Munez was able to forge new relations with her staff. The basic respect required for positive relationships had been restored. Many teachers liked her and she them. Most teachers even had positive impressions of her competence and integrity. However, Mrs. Munez had still not begun to really accomplish projects with her faculty as partners. She continued to direct, and they continued to work in their classrooms. Without more high-risk interactions that involved working together, the impressions of competence and integrity did not grow into more solid discernments. What's more, the strong-handed leadership coupled with frequent staff turnover created some feelings of vulnerability among the teachers in which they began to be afraid to openly communicate with the principal.

The lack of delegated authority affected teacher-teacher relationships as well. The elimination of perceptions of prejudice among staff and the restoration of basic respect allowed teachers to begin to develop perceptions of personal regard with each other. However, the troubled past in the school precluded any tradition of teachers meeting for social functions, and Mrs. Munez did not put forth special effort to change this. In addition, because she did not delegate authority, teachers were not put together professionally to work on important school policy matters. A new teacher reported, "We're social with one another, but there's not a lot of time for more." Another new teacher complained that the faculty operated mostly as cliques. She found that professional support from her fellow teachers was not always there: "I'm new to teaching a class. I need help. Most are helpful if questioned. About 20% aren't. They say they have no time." Thus, although there was a marked improvement in teacher-teacher trust due to the removal of divisive personalities, trust between teachers remained low overall.

The principal's great effort to develop a base of support among parents involved many successful low-risk interactions with positive discernments of respect and personal regard between the principal and parents. One veteran teacher noted, "She has a good rapport [with the parents]. They are glad to have her. She is their voice in the school." Mrs. Munez's focus on the children and implementation of programs concerning safety and nutrition presumably also led to positive discernments of her integrity and competence among most parents and a growth of trust overall in the relationship.

However, the role for parents at Mills was still quite limited. The principal created formal positions on committees and helped parents get elected to the local school board. Yet, in practice, these parents did not act as partners with the principal in doing the work of the school. At times, they appeared to be her subordinates, reporting to her on a group's activities. Other times, they quietly gave their approval to her proposals with minimal explanation. While this limited role for parents may have been in part due to Mrs. Munez's strong-handed leadership style, it may also have been related to a lack of confidence among parents to take on important policy decisions on schooling due to their lack of education or their cultural understandings of their appropriate role in schooling. Whatever the reason, without working together in more high-risk interactions, parents at Mills were not able to form more complete discernments of the principal's competence and integrity, and the trust between parents and principal could not advance further.

Changes in school policy and staffing brought respect back to parent-teacher interactions. Teachers were generally positive when talking about parents at Mills. One newer teacher noted, "This is a nice community. Most get along well." Still a veteran teacher complained about the lack of parent involvement: "We're not working to capacity. Parents aren't working with their kids at home." A newer colleague suggested that relations between teachers and parents were hampered by the language barrier: "Parents still help with the kids, but most are working. Some will change their days off to help in the classroom. But there are some divisions. . . . It's a bit divisive because of the language issue." Another teacher suggested that the lack of involvement was due to differences in the cultural understandings of roles in schooling. "Families don't question me. I think it's cultural—that they don't question the teacher." Whether due to education, language, or culture, the lack of high-risk interaction between teachers and parents around the work of the school impeded the growth of trust.

SUMMARY

By the year 2000, trust at Mills had grown in some role-set relations but languished in others. Consortium trust measures show that trust between the teachers and principal grew significantly between 1997 and 1999, going from well below the systemwide average to just above average. Trust among teachers, however, failed to increase and remained well below average. The measure of trust between teachers and parents is the most troubling at Mills. In this case, trust actually fell between 1997 and 1999, from a level near the system average to a below-average level.

Mrs. Munez began her tenure with trust at an abysmal level. She set the stage for the formation of trust relationships by pushing out divisive personalities, promoting her vision that the needs of the children come first, and creating opportunities for low-risk interactions between herself and the teachers and parents. These changes also restored basic respect to relations among teachers and between teachers and parents. However, five years into her principalship at Mills, Mrs. Munez had not yet implemented formal changes in the school to promote more high-risk interaction between herself and the teachers and parents, between individual teachers, or between teachers and parents. Therefore, the growth of trust stalled at Mills and positive perceptions of competence and integrity could not develop.

MacNeil and Mills present opposite extremes when looking at the base conditions of trust. As such, they suggest how the proposed theory of trust building might be used differently according to the initial level of trust. With a strong level of trust already established, Dr. Wilson was able to implement strategies that put people to work together immediately to further develop the trust relationships. Mrs. Munez, however, was forced to concentrate on strategies that eased vulnerabilities and initiated low-risk interactions. Attempts to promote more high-risk interactions initially would have aggravated the unease and distrust. While the low levels of trust at Mills required a concentration of efforts to set the stage for trust building and engage people in low-risk interactions, by the end of the study, Mrs. Munez's disregard for providing opportunities for higher-risk interactions caused the overall level of trust to plateau. Indeed, if conditions continued, one might see an eventual decline in trust at Mills, especially between the principal and teachers.

5 Cole Magnet Elementary School

Coming Back to Trust

As part of a 1980 federal consent decree, the City of Chicago opened several magnet schools designed to better integrate schools by attracting White students to public schools outside their neighborhoods. This group of schools had to maintain a student-body racial composition of 15–35% White and 65–85% non-White. (Due to racial changes in the city-wide student body, the goal of at least 15% White students per magnet school was no longer feasible by mid-1990 and not met by many of the schools.) In general, magnet schools were given extra resources to operate special programs that would attract students from across the city. Admission to the schools was determined by lottery drawings. In 1998, the city modified its magnet school policy to set aside 30% of seats in magnet schools for neighborhood children and to provide busing for students living outside the neighborhood but within a six-mile radius of the school.

Cole Magnet Elementary is one of the original magnet schools in Chicago, created in response to the 1980 consent decree. It is situated in a neighborhood of manicured lawns and 1950s suburban-style housing on the south side of Chicago. The neighborhood was then and continues to be populated by upper middle-class Black families. Even before the change in public school policy that called for a neighborhood allowance, Cole Magnet drew students heavily from nearby families. At the beginning of the 1990s, the school's racial composition was 73% Black, 15% White, and 12% other minorities. Demographic changes citywide combined with changes in the magnet policy moved the racial composition to over 93% Black by the end of the decade, with only 1% White and 6% other minorities. Over this same time period, the percentage of low-income students remained fairly steady, with around 45% of the student body accepting free or reduced lunches in the year 2000.

The combination of a high concentration of Black students and low percentage of students from low-income families made Cole Magnet an unusual exception to most Chicago public schools. Its magnet program was succeeding in attracting middle- and upper-class Black families. As a result, the school staff was dealing with a special group of parents, one that was especially motivated in that they sought out a better school for their children. In addition, this parent group was highly educated and had resources that could be useful to the school.

Cole Magnet was also unusual because of its extremely small size. The school served fewer than 300 students, thus needing only two classrooms per grade. Even given the small number of students, by the 1990s Cole Magnet was struggling with space issues. While soliciting capital funding from the central office for an addition, the school located vacant space several miles northeast of the main building to house their primary grades. Thus, Grades K–3 were moved to "the annex" and continued to be there at the end of the decade while funding was still being sought.

As with many magnet schools, the extra resources of the school and the students' families resulted in consistently high test scores. Throughout the 1990s, around 70% of the students at Cole Magnet scored at or above national norms in both reading and math. In some years, this percentage dipped below seventy. In other years, it went as high as 75%. However, there appeared to be no trend, either up or down, during this time span.

A TEMPORARY INTRUSION

In the early 1990s, Cole Magnet hired Lynn Chadwick as principal. A first-time principal, Ms. Chadwick was eager to succeed at Cole Magnet and prove herself to the central office administrators. As such, she came to the school looking to implement change. One priority was to upgrade the physical plant of the school so that it could handle the technology available then and in the future. She wanted computers in every classroom with data and communication lines to make them useful. She also wanted her teaching staff to be adept at using the technology in their curricula. Thus, her second priority was to push the faculty to adopt new teaching strategies.

As a third priority, Ms. Chadwick focused her attention on making full use of the resources of her parent group. First, she wanted to boost attendance at the local school council (LSC) meetings. To do so, she structured LSC meetings to include dinners prepared and served by rotating pairs of teachers and the presentation of individual awards for an outstanding student at each grade level. Second, she pushed the parent-teacher organization (PTO) to set a goal of recruiting 100% of the families at Cole Magnet into their membership.

While many of the teachers at Cole Magnet appreciated the technological upgrades brought in by Ms. Chadwick, some resented her interference in matters of instruction. Most of the faculty members at the school were veteran teachers who had been producing students with high test scores for years. As one teacher recalls, some veteran teachers found Ms. Chadwick's leadership style to be intrusive:

> [Ms. Chadwick] was very hands on. It made it a little harder. There were some confrontations. . . . You're talking to a large group of veteran teachers who had had extremely good results. She wanted to change things. . . . Because of personality conflicts, a lot of people became eligible [for retirement] who could have worked for another ten years but opted out early.

Thus, Ms. Chadwick was forced to replace one third of her teaching staff due to early retirements.

Throughout Ms. Chadwick's tenure at Cole Magnet, Thomas Truman served as assistant principal. Hired into the position by the previous principal, Mr. Truman had been a teacher at Cole Magnet for more than fifteen years. A friendly person with an easy smile, teachers and students both responded positively to Mr. Truman's low-key manner. Many colleagues remarked on his clear dedication to the children. One teacher noted, "He's really trying to do what's best for the children. He's very much involved with the children. He'll stop and speak to them and call them by name."

Thus, when Ms. Chadwick was promoted to a position in the central office, the faculty and staff at Cole Magnet thought that Mr. Truman was a natural fit as principal. In fact, Mr. Truman had served as interim principal before Ms. Chadwick had been hired and then again once she resigned her position. One teacher recalled the hiring process: "Many of the teachers were supportive of Mr. Truman. So we got together and drafted a letter of support. As assistant principal, he was very good at what he did. So, we thought, 'Let's continue.'" The members of the local school board did consider other candidates, but in the end they agreed to promote Mr. Truman.

RETURNING TO NORMAL:
THE MAINTENANCE PRINCIPAL

As principal at Cole Magnet, Mr. Truman continued to communicate the same vision of schooling he had as assistant principal—that of acting in the best interest of the children. In both roles, he often used symbolic leadership to convey his beliefs. A warm man who tried to put everyone at ease, Mr. Truman made visitors feel welcome at the school. One teacher remarked on the amount of time he spent interacting with the children rather than working in his office: "He stands in front of the building, greeting kids as they get off the bus. I'm sure there's a bunch of paperwork waiting for him inside. You see him carrying bags of it home after school." Another teacher noted, "He takes time out to really talk to the children. He knows them personally." As Mr. Truman explained, even his choice of wearing a dress shirt and tie every day was a conscious decision to be a role model as a Black, male professional for his mostly Black student body.

Mr. Truman's major policy change from the previous principal was to leave teachers to do their work. He treated them as professionals who were capable of doing their jobs. He noted, "They're a good staff, and they know what they are doing. I try to clear the way for them to do what they do in the classroom." One teacher recognized the change: "He's the kind of individual who gives you the respect you deserve. He gives you a job and expects you to do it." Teachers at Cole Magnet already worked together through the formal structures of grade-level meetings and small-group committees. Because there were only two teachers per grade level, these meetings consisted of at least two grades to help bring continuity across grades in the curriculum and to give teachers more than one person's feedback on issues that might arise. In addition to the multi-grade-level meetings, the school maintained several committees that met on important school policy matters, such as curriculum, discipline, and school climate. These committees were formed around the issues identified by an earlier school improvement plan, and each teacher belonged to two committees, with membership rotating every year.

Mr. Truman continued to use the existing formal structures that brought teachers together to work on policy and instruction. In addition, he created an open-door policy for them to work with him. One veteran teacher noted his receptive manner: "He will listen. The door is always open." Even more, he often actively sought out their input for decision making. One teacher recalled that Mr. Truman used the committee and grade-level meeting structure as well as informal conversations to gather information. Then he brought together the many viewpoints to form policy: "Mr. Truman would make the final decision, but it was based on the teacher input."

Using his easy manner and a good sense of diplomacy, Mr. Truman acted as a buffer when conflicts arose between teachers and parents and between individual teachers. He noted that his first priority was to remind everyone that they are all working for the best interests of the kids. One teacher talked about Mr. Truman's ability to handle the parents: "He's very accommodating. He'll try the best he can to solve their problems. He'll be honest with the parents." Another teacher noted his facilitative style when dealing with issues within the school: "He anticipates problems and tries to address them. If the teachers aren't in sync on a particular idea, he'll say, 'Come on, come on. Let's have a talk.'"

To further promote communication at the school, Mr. Truman began to fill vacancies with people who might help him bridge the distance between the two buildings. He hired a well-liked, upper-level teacher as assistant principal. The new assistant principal, Mr. O'Leary, matched Mr. Truman's friendly, easygoing manner. While the two administrators tried to spend time at both buildings, Mr. O'Leary was primarily stationed at the annex and Mr. Truman at the main school.

In addition to the new assistant principal, Mr. Truman was eventually able to hire one of the primary-grade teachers, Mrs. Kucek, as the instructional coordinator. He planned to use the position to bring continuity among the teachers across the two buildings. Because it was difficult for the two groups of teachers to meet together physically, Mr. Truman hoped the instructional coordinator could meet with each group separately and carry on a dialogue from one group to the next. An energetic and talkative woman who found it easy to put a positive spin on things, Mrs. Kucek was a good fit for the job.

Despite the changes in leadership style and the hiring of new administrators, Mr. Truman's strategy was mostly one of keeping the status quo. As one veteran teacher noted, "The previous principal made many, many changes and did lots of things. I would say Mr. Truman, more than being innovative, has been a maintenance principal." After the turbulent years of Ms. Chadwick's tenure, many teachers viewed this strategy positively. One teacher stated that there was little need for change because the school functioned well: "I think that there were things that were set in motion that he just continued. . . . I think it was more to go with what was comfortable, what was working, to keep what was working in place."

SHARED GOVERNANCE, FACILITATED RELATIONSHIPS, AND A LACK OF DIRECTION

As Mr. Truman assumed the role of principal at Cole Magnet, most role relationships in the school were characterized by some degree of trust.

With a staff of seventeen grade-level teachers divided between the main school and the annex into groups of ten and seven, respectively, Cole Magnet's small size facilitated the growth of positive relationships among the teachers. Teachers found it easy to communicate often and form personal bonds with the other teachers in their building. One teacher described the school staff as a "family." Another teacher described their relationships as strong enough to endure conflict: "People may have disagreements, but they stay involved with each other. They still work to give ideas and advice and to get ideas and advice."

The formal grade-level and committee structures provided a format in which teachers might form positive discernments of their colleagues' competence and integrity. In fact, teachers at Cole Magnet often talked glowingly of their confidence in the competence of their colleagues. Matters of integrity were discussed less often. Teachers seemed to assume that their colleagues were motivated to do what was in the best interest of the children. Several times, teachers talked about differences in instructional styles as disagreements over what would help the children the most. One teacher described her colleagues as "very competent." She went on to explain, "There are learning styles just like teaching styles. They all do it differently." Another teacher noted, "The concern for the children is there, but I do see some methods of instruction that might need a little fine-tuning."

Thus, within each building, trust among the teachers was high. However, the two groups of teachers had little opportunity to interact. Faculty meetings were held separately with the assistant principal at the annex and the principal at the main building. The two faculties never had a chance to meet together except on days that the children were not in school. Teachers often noted this separation as a challenge for communication and continuity. One teacher remarked that having two campuses was difficult for the students as well: "The transition from third to fourth grade is harder. Also, students in reading and math who are working at a higher level can't walk to the next grade for that lesson." Similarly, teachers from the annex were unable to meet with their colleagues at the main building for informal advice and support.

The many curriculum and instruction changes instituted by Ms. Chadwick were interpreted by teachers as attacks on their competence. New to the school and eager to succeed, Ms. Chadwick began implementing reforms without first establishing even a base of respect and personal regard with the teachers. Policy changes were not a result of working with the teachers but rather came from the principal and were directed at the teachers. Thus, trust between the teachers and principal fell drastically during her tenure as principal. As Mr. Truman assumed the role, trust in this role relationship had already begun to rise in that many teachers shared mutual respect and personal regard with him and had positive discernments of his competence and integrity as assistant principal.

During Ms. Chadwick's tenure, teachers and parents enjoyed mutual respect and positive discernments of each other's integrity. As one teacher noted, the efforts parents expended to get their children into a magnet school demonstrated that they were concerned about education: "As a magnet school, we have children here whose parents have chosen to have them here. In that sense, you have a considerably more interested group of parents." Because most students were bused to and from the school, teachers and parents had little opportunity to see one another on a daily, informal basis to develop positive discernments of personal regard. Some teachers stated that most of their parents worked during the school day and therefore could not volunteer in their classrooms. As one teacher noted, teachers and parents often did not see one another unless a conflict arose: "A lot of times people come when there's a problem. And that's the only time they focus on the teacher." Another teacher found that parents were not always supportive of the teachers in these conflicts: "I think that sometimes when there's a problem, the parents take the student's side." In addition, some teachers felt that parents sometimes intruded into their domain, the work of the classroom, by pushing teachers to change the curriculum: "Sometimes they put more on them than is really age appropriate for their physical, mental, and emotional health."

Overall, however, most teachers viewed these situations as typical parental concern. One teacher noted that she did not believe parents were questioning the school staff's competence in these conflicts: "I believe parents trust this school, trust it safety wise, trust it educationally. . . . There are always some confrontations." Another teacher discussed how these conflicts were quickly resolved. "There have been times when parents have protested a student's grades. . . . But then it comes to a parent meeting, and it'll get solved."

Similar to the relationship between parents and teachers, the relationship between the parents at Cole Magnet and Ms. Chadwick was characterized by mutual respect and mostly positive discernments of competence and integrity. Some teachers reported that the principal maintained a "good rapport" with parents and kept her door open to them. While Ms. Chadwick instituted efforts to significantly increase ties between the parents and the school, she did not have the kind of warm personality that easily led to more personal interactions with parents. Thus, the relationships remained professional and were not characterized by personal regard.

At the time he took over as principal at Cole Magnet, Mr. Truman already had trusting relationships established with the teachers and parents. As assistant principal, he articulated a vision of schooling that put the needs of the children first. He used symbolic leadership to convey that vision and gained positive discernments of his integrity from both teachers and parents. He treated others with respect in his daily interactions and showed personal regard by caring for teachers and parents as a friend. As principal, he continued to do these things. Already viewed as a competent assistant principal, Mr. Truman raised the level of trust between teachers and the principal just by taking over the position.

Trust between the teachers at Cole Magnet continued to be high during Mr. Truman's tenure. However, the lack of direct interaction between the two buildings continued to be a problem. As one teacher noted, the two faculties needed to be together to work together as a school: "We're all friends, but we're not all one." Another teacher reported that the lack of resolution to the problem was beginning to affect trust between the teachers and the principal: "He had a high level of trust, but then problems occur which they always do with a faculty over two schools. . . . Because it's hard for him to be in both places."

Trust between the teachers and parents increased during Mr. Truman's tenure in part due to his facilitative leadership style. Parents continued to question teachers on matters of instruction. At one local school board meeting, one parent raised a concern that the level of Spanish vocabulary her child had to learn was too difficult. She cited specific examples of words that she thought were too advanced for a second grader. Mr. Truman addressed the woman's concerns immediately. He noted that this type of issue was exactly why he had appointed Mrs. Kucek as instructional coordinator. He asked that the parent set up a meeting with Mrs. Kucek (who was there) so that they could further discuss the issue. While treating the parent's concerns with respect and sincerity, he also protected his teachers from intrusion by allowing Mrs. Kucek to negotiate grievances with the curriculum and pass any changes on to the teacher in a more positive light.

Some teachers, however, were beginning to see a drop in parent participation in the school. It was difficult to get volunteers in the classroom. Attendance at local school board meetings was dropping. Teachers wanted to see parents in the school more. One teacher talked about how important parent support was to the school:

> I would say parents are supportive, but not as much as in years past. . . . We'd like to go back to a school contract where they would sign that they understand the responsibilities of having their child in school and what they can do to help. . . . Some parents can become wonderful allies. I would like to see it increase. . . . I think that it's fallen off, but I don't think it's a lost cause.

Thus, while the buffer between teachers and parents helped increase positive discernments of respect, personal regard, competence, and integrity, the decrease in interaction that was either purely social or that included working together on a project might eventually hinder the growth of trust.

Overall, Mr. Truman's strategy as a maintenance principal, while successful in the short term, became a problem for trust relations as his tenure went on. Just as some teachers were looking for new ways to work with the parents, other teachers felt they needed to work more with their colleagues on professional development. Some teachers talked of problems of curricular continuity and increasing teacher performance. One teacher noted, "I do feel it's time that we bring in new programs. We've kind of been on a plateau for a couple of years." Most teachers still held positive discernments of their colleagues' competence and integrity, but without working together on a schoolwide improvement initiative it was difficult for those positive discernments to continue indefinitely. Even successful veteran teachers must be seen as striving to hone their craft rather than resting on past laurels for colleagues to perceive them as acting with integrity. Thus, while the formal structures to work together were in place, teachers needed Mr. Truman to facilitate a discussion on how the school was going to improve rather than merely stay with what was working.

SUMMARY

Cole Magnet saw an increase in trust between the teachers and the principal and between the teachers and the parents during Mr. Truman's initial years as principal. Consortium measures showed a dramatic increase in teacher-principal trust from an above-average level in 1997 to an extremely high level in 1999. Teacher-parent trust also experienced significant growth, even though the school started with a level in the top quartile of the system in 1997. Teacher-teacher trust was the only category that did not experience significant growth, although it remained well above average throughout the time period.

Mr. Truman set the stage for this growth in trust simply by articulating his vision of education. Working with a competent staff that already acted in the best interests of the children, Mr. Truman had no need to reshape the faculty. Trust between the principal and the teachers and parents was already high. By giving the teachers more freedom on matters of instruction, he further increased trust between the teachers and the principal. The structures for teachers and parents to interact were already in place. Mr. Truman only had to fine-tune them by acting as a buffer between the two groups so that everyone could agree that they were all working for the children. Teachers already worked well together and had the structures in place to do so. However, the case study revealed that two years beyond the last Consortium measures, many relationships were being negatively affected by a lack of effort to improve the school, with an emphasis on simply maintaining the status quo.

As a final case, Cole Magnet presents an interesting contrast to both MacNeil and Mills. Unlike Mills, the faculty at Cole Magnet had well-developed relationships based on mutual respect and personal regard. In contrast to MacNeil, the teachers also had well-developed professional relationships based on perceptions of competence and integrity. While Cole Magnet had relatively high levels of trust across all role relations under the previous principal, teachers had actually experienced a decline in trust with the principal. Therefore, the new principal was able to restore a positive state of relations by acting in the best interest of the children and allowing teachers to return to the shared governance they had previously experienced. The positive, social relationships among teachers and between teachers and Mr. Truman required no new efforts to encourage more successful, low-risk interactions as seen at Mills. With formal opportunities for high-risk interactions and positive relationships already in place, the principal at Cole Magnet had no need to undertake the same kind of policy changes and development of a professional community as seen at MacNeil.

The relationship between the parents and the school professionals at Cole Magnet was also quite different from those at MacNeil and Mills. Cole Magnet had a very powerful and proactive parent base. However, the presence of busing and parental work schedules prevented frequent low-risk, social interactions between the parents and teachers. While perceptions of competence and integrity were generally positive, most parent-teacher interaction occurred only when conflicts arose about curricular content, student grades, or behavior problems. As such, rather than focusing efforts on increasing parental participation as at MacNeil and Mills, Mr. Truman concentrated on creating a buffer to help parents and teachers come to common understandings about the work of the school.

In many respects, Cole Magnet appears to be the ideal high-trust school. However, because the study observed the school as it maintained trust relationships, rather than witnessing efforts to build trust relationships, Cole Magnet provides an interesting insight into trust not previously discussed in the research on trust building. The case study of Cole Magnet along with the Consortium trust measures provide evidence that Mr. Truman's lack of interference with teachers and negotiation between parents and teachers helped increase perceptions of trust across adult relations in the school. However, the case study also noted concerns among teachers about the lack of focused direction for the school. Some teachers worried that their colleagues weren't all on the same page. Others talked about a need to continually improve the quality of teaching in the school. While the formal structures for shared governance functioned quite well at Cole Magnet, the teachers wanted more guidance from their principal in setting a schoolwide agenda for improvement. In a sense, Mr. Truman had limited his role with the teachers to that of administrator and colleague. Some teachers were asking him to also be a leader.

6

An Examination of Trust Building Through Quantitative Analyses

As educators, we know that trust is important when we're trying to improve our schools. The previous chapters went a long way toward describing how to build trust in schools. We know from the literature on trust that we need to ease vulnerabilities by setting the stage for trust and promoting low-risk interactions and then continue to bring people together through more high-risk interactions. The case studies showed how this model of trust building operates in the everyday workings of the school. In addition, the cases provided some insights into how the model might operate differently in different contexts. The insights from our cases raise four hypotheses:

1. The base state of trust influences which strategies are most effective in building trust.

2. In schools with growing trust between parents and teachers, the formal structures for parental involvement vary with the economic and education level of the parents.

3. When the parent base is active, the principal must act as a buffer between parents and teachers to build trust between the two groups.

4. The same interactions that foster trust between the principal and teachers promotes trust between the teachers.

While these hypotheses are clearly demonstrated by our cases, we cannot assume that they will hold true in other urban schools. Therefore, we should test them with a larger data set so that we can have more confidence in our understanding of how trust building really works.

To explore our four hypotheses, I used data collected by the Consortium on Chicago School Research from elementary school teacher and principal surveys administered in 1997 and 1999. The Consortium surveys include items on instructional methods, school leadership, teacher collegiality, parent involvement and community relations, school climate, relations with the Central Office of the Board of Education, and participation with external partners in educational improvement (Sebring et al., 1995). Although the survey items and themes have been honed over the years to better address the concepts being studied, the Consortium has produced a set of measures that are comparable across the surveys. Included in these measures are three trust measures from teacher reports on the relationships between teachers and parents, between teachers and their principal, and between individual teachers in a school. These measures and the items that comprise them are listed in Resource A.

In addition to the trust measures, there are other measures and items that can be used to represent some mechanisms of trust building in our model, such as reports from teachers on the principal's communication of a belief system that puts children first, daily informal interactions among teachers, daily informal interactions between school staff and parents, the principal's modeling of behavior for the teachers, teachers' belief in a school mission that puts children first, teachers efforts to put an instructional program together, teachers' reflection on their practices together, and teachers' participation in shared decision making. There are also measures and items from principal reports to indicate a principal reshaping the faculty and teachers sharing in a school mission that puts children first. In addition to the survey data, census data and demographic data are used in many analyses to make the results representative across all schools, regardless of differences in racial composition, socioeconomic status, or prior achievement of the student body.

HOW DOES A LOW BASE STATE OF TRUST AFFECT THE EFFECTIVENESS OF TRUST-BUILDING STRATEGIES?

The case studies of MacNeil, Mills, and Cole Magnet help bring to life the mechanisms for trust building described in Chapter 2. In addition, they highlight how differences in the base state of trust might affect which strategies are most useful for trust building. The contrasting base states of

MacNeil and Mills resulted in contrasting strategies for the two principals. The principal at MacNeil, the high-trust school, invested much of her time and energy in formalizing opportunities for successful, high-risk interactions, whereas the principal at Mills, the low-trust school, remained focused on easing vulnerabilities.

As noted in the discussion of the theory, many of the mechanisms suggested for promoting positive, high-risk interactions are not likely to work well without some level of trust already present. Without a base of positive social interaction characterized by respect and personal regard, formal structures such as shared decision making and peer evaluation can heighten vulnerabilities rather than increasing trust. Indeed, if teachers with a high sense of vulnerability were asked to work on building a school strategy together, the meetings might devolve into fractious arguments or go on without meaningful participation, debate, or buy-in. Thus, it is worthwhile to explore whether the base state of trust affects the usefulness of different types of mechanisms in building trust in schools other than those in our case studies.

The case studies lead us to believe that if trust is low, more time must be spent on easing vulnerabilities rather than promoting high-risk interactions. Analyses conducted on the bottom 25% of schools on the trust measures in the Chicago sample (about seventy schools) suggest that the mechanisms involved in setting the stage for trust and promoting low-risk interactions are linked to a growth of trust over time. The ability of the principal to reshape the faculty, a key mechanism in setting the stage for trust, is a significant predictor of the growth of trust between teachers and the principal as well as between teachers and parents. In addition, the principal communicating a vision that puts children first, the other key mechanism in setting the stage, is a significant predictor of the growth of trust between teachers and the principal. Finally, the results show that the presence of informal, social events among teachers, a low-risk interaction, is a significant predictor of growing trust among teachers in these low-trust schools. In all analyses, teachers sharing a common school mission is the only high-risk mechanism that predicted a growth of trust, and it did so only for teacher-teacher trust.

Overall, the empirical analyses on the Chicago sample suggest that schools starting with a low base state of trust must spend more time on mechanisms that set the stage for trust and promote successful, low-risk interactions, rather than on those that promote more high-risk interactions. Therefore, school professionals in low-trust environments must invest more effort into mechanisms that ease vulnerabilities, such as social activities; easily accomplished projects; communication of a common vision; small-group meetings; and positive, daily interactions.

IN SCHOOLS WITH GROWING PARENT-TEACHER TRUST, HOW DOES PARENT INVOLVEMENT VARY WITH THE ECONOMIC LEVEL OF THE PARENTS?

The case studies of Mills and MacNeil provide an interesting contrast regarding the role of the parents in the school. Both schools were successful in building trust between parents and school professionals, but they used very different activity levels to get there. At MacNeil, the teachers and principal developed more ways to include the parents in the work of the school. The institution of parent approval of daily agendas assured a minimum level of participation and awareness of classroom activities for all parents. The increase in special social events organized around the work of the school, such as family math night, brought many parents into the school in a relaxed, social manner. The creation of committee seats and staff positions to be filled by parents gave some parents a true partnership in helping to shape the work of the school.

However, the Mills case showed a parent base that was mostly inactive when it came to the work of the school. In fact, at the beginning of the current principal's tenure, the Hispanic parents were not represented by even a single seat on the local school council (LSC). Rather, politically active community members had mobilized to fill the local school board with opponents of the Hispanic migration into the community. The principal spent much of her time and effort galvanizing a support base among the Hispanic parents so that the school could address the needs of their children rather than maintaining efforts to push them out of the community. Indeed, much of the work of the principal with the parents revolved around the school providing them with resources on parenting and community development. By the end of the study, there were parents filling positions on the LSC. However, they fulfilled their duties without a true sense of authority or partnership. The principal provided an overview of the actions she was taking that required their vote, and they overwhelmingly voted to approve the issues—without discussion or questions.

The differing roles for the parents in the cases parallel differences in economic and educational levels of the school communities. MacNeil was situated in a middle-class community that was experiencing an immigration of wealthier, highly educated families. Mills was located in a community of low-income immigrants. Therefore, a second lesson from the cases may be that the formal structures created for parent involvement will vary with the economic and education level of the parents. Schools serving low-income, low-education level families will need to develop their parental resources before their inclusion on committees is effective. In such cases, more time may be spent on increasing communication between home and school or including parents on social committee work rather than including them on more significant committees. Schools that have a highly educated parent base can more easily recruit parents for significant committees involving school leadership and will receive useful input from those parents. Schools without that base may need to work to recruit parents, and often those parents are unable to make significant contributions on these committees due to either a lack of knowledge about the issues or a lack of confidence to question the opinions of the professional staff of the school.

To explore the relationship between parent involvement and income further, an empirical analysis was conducted on the top 25% of schools with a growth in trust between teachers and parents in the Chicago sample (about eighty-five schools). In this analysis, the level of poverty in the school community was correlated with a survey measure of parental involvement. The level of poverty in the community as used in this analysis is simply a crude approximation of parent education and ability levels. The parental involvement measure consisted of survey items asking teachers how many of their parents participate in various activities, including report card pickup, teacher-parent conferences, special events, school fundraising activities, and classroom volunteer opportunities. A higher value on the measure would indicate that parents are not only involved in more activities but are also involved in more high-risk activities (e.g., volunteering and fundraising vs. report card pickup).

The correlation analysis shows a highly significant, negative relationship between the concentration of poverty and the level of parental involvement in schools with growing trust between teachers and parents, which lends support to the second hypothesis. That is, among schools with growing teacher-parent trust, the level of parental involvement goes down and increasingly consists of activities that are less risky as the concentration of poverty in a school community goes up.

We have to be careful when looking at these results. Remember, all the schools in this analysis are high-trust schools. Therefore, it isn't the case that greater parental involvement in the form of higher-risk activities simply leads to higher levels of trust. Rather, these results suggest that the types of activities we use to make up parental involvement vary with the types of communities we are serving and that both low- and high-risk activities can be used to build trust. It is more likely that the parents' support of the work of the school affects the growth of trust rather than their ability to become involved in more high-risk ways. The introduction of high-risk activities is important for the growth of trust with parents when the parent population is prepared to engage in more high-risk activities, such as committee work. However, low-risk activities, such as social events and positive, informal interactions, can be effective in building trust with populations that are less prepared to become actively involved in the work of the school. School professionals must design their parent involvement efforts to meet the ability level of their parents.

HOW IMPORTANT IS A BUFFER BETWEEN TEACHERS AND PARENTS IN SCHOOLS WHERE PARENTAL INVOLVEMENT IS STRONG?

The role of the parents at Cole Magnet provides another interesting observation about relations between parents and school professionals. At Cole Magnet, the parent base was active, with access to many resources. Parents often discussed matters of curriculum and instruction with the professional staff of the school. This type of involvement in the work of the school appeared to be accepted by teachers. None of those interviewed questioned the validity of the parents delving into what is typically the domain of the faculty. However, the teachers felt uneasy during the tenure of the previous principal, who was more likely to question matters of curriculum and instruction rather than support a teacher when questions from the parents arose. During this period, the teachers did not object to the parents' questions as much as the lack of assurance by the principal that everyone involved was a professional who had the children's best interests at heart. The new principal provided this background understanding to disagreements between teachers and parents. He acted as a buffer for the teachers so that they were comfortable making changes to please the parents without feeling that their competence and integrity were being questioned. Is the role of the principal as a buffer important at other schools with high levels of parental involvement as well?

To examine the role of the principal as a buffer, empirical analyses were conducted on the top 25% of schools with high parent involvement in the Chicago sample (about eighty-five schools). Principals were tagged as "buffer principals" if they reported that mistrust between teachers and parents was not a problem if they reported on teacher reports that theirs was a top school, that the principal promoted parent and community involvement, and that the school's relations with parents and the community had been getting better over the past two years. The results of the analyses found a weakly significant relationship between the presence of a buffer principal and the growth of trust between teachers and parents in schools with high levels of parental involvement. It appears that a buffer principal could be important in schools with an active parent base. A better set of survey questions might bring stronger results to support this hypothesis.

Hence, principals might mediate relationships between parents and teachers to benefit the growth of trust between the two groups. Principals can establish boundaries for interactions between teachers and parents, keeping parents from treading on areas of teaching expertise and helping teachers establish effective ways to communicate their views to parents. As the intermediary, a principal can ease interactions simply by taming harsh words or repackaging criticism into more helpful terms. Most important, as in the case of Cole Magnet, principals can reaffirm for all parties that they are working toward the same goal, making professionalism and care for the children part of the shared culture of the school.

DOES THE GROWTH OF TEACHER-PRINCIPAL TRUST LEAD TO A GROWTH IN TEACHER-TEACHER TRUST?

In that the theory of trust building put forth in this study evolved from the principal leadership literature, there is support for the hypothesis that the mechanisms involved in setting the stage, promoting low-risk interactions, and blending in more high-risk interactions are part of the development of trust between the principal and the teachers and the principal and parents. However, there is no similar guidance in the literature about building trust within the faculty and between the teachers and parents. Observations from the case studies indicate that many of the same mechanisms that were used to build trust between the principal and teachers were also useful in building trust between the teachers. For example, teachers who were engaged in discussion about the mission with the principal may also have been building trust among themselves by engaging in interactions with respect and personal regard and demonstrating their competence and integrity. When a principal acted to reduce the vulnerability of the teachers, they became more open to engaging in positive interactions with their colleagues as well as the principal. When teachers engaged as a group in successful activities with the principal, they were also working with one another and building similar trust relationships among teachers as between the principal and teachers. Therefore, let's examine whether the efforts a principal uses to promote teacher-principal trust also establish a climate that is likely to promote the growth of trust within a faculty.

To explore this relationship, a set of empirical analyses was conducted on all schools in the Chicago sample (about 375 schools). The findings show that the growth of trust between teachers and principal has a positive, significant relationship with the growth of trust between teachers. The results suggest that the growth of trust between different role relationships is related. In other words, the same activities that are used to promote the growth of teacher-principal trust will likely have a positive impact on the growth of teacher-teacher trust.

This is good news for school administrators. By focusing on building a relationship between the principal and the faculty, a principal can also build relationships between faculty members. It makes sense when we look at the mechanisms involved. Reshaping the faculty not only communicates a principal's competence and integrity, but it also creates a more cohesive faculty. Communicating a vision of schooling that puts the needs of the children first not only presents a principal's beliefs that teachers can easily agree with, but it also establishes a school vision that is easily shared among faculty members. The mechanisms of high-risk interaction especially affect relationships between teachers along with trust between teachers and principal. For example, when a principal shares power, he or she must put teachers to work together. This provides more opportunities for positive perceptions of competence and integrity among teachers. In the end, strategies that help build trust between the principal and the faculty provide the same opportunities to build trust between and among faculty members.

SUMMARY

The above analyses show support for the hypotheses derived from the case studies. First, principals in low-trust schools are more likely to find the mechanisms in setting the stage and promoting successful, low-risk exchanges effective in building trust than by using the mechanisms that promote successful, high-risk exchanges. Second, the types of parent involvement used to promote the growth of teacher-parent trust vary with the types of resources parents may be able to bring to the school. Third, teacher-parent trust is more likely to grow in schools with high levels of parental involvement if the principal acts as a buffer. Finally, the growth of trust between teachers is related to the growth of teacher-principal trust.

7 Implementing Trust-Building Strategies in Your School

I n the media, in all levels of government, and in our homes, school reform is often the topic of discussion. The debates frequently focus on raising teacher competency or instituting new teaching methodologies. Some argue that the curriculum must be expanded. Others want to go back to basics. As a nation, we want to identify our best and brightest students and allow them to excel. However, we also want our schools to prepare all our children well for entry into adulthood. In the midst of these debates and their attendant reform efforts remain the principals, teachers, students, and their parents who must continue to carry on the work of schooling, whatever the latest trend.

While the choice of curriculum matters and the type of instructional method is important, people are at the heart of schooling. No matter how innovative a school reform may be, it is unlikely to succeed unless the people on the front lines of schooling are working well together to implement it. In the past few years, research has found links between the growth of relational trust and positive organizational outcomes that are likely to benefit school improvement efforts. Studies have shown that a growth in trust predicts a growth in teacher commitment to the school and a greater openness to innovation (Bryk & Schneider, 1996, 2002). The latest work on trust in schools ties the growth of trust to gains in school productivity or increased student achievement (Bryk & Schneider, 2002; Goddard, Tschannen-Moran & Hoy, 2001). Thus, the relationships between principals, teachers, and parents cannot be ignored when attempting school reform.

WHICH STRATEGIES ARE
EFFECTIVE IN BUILDING TRUST?

The model put forth in this book begins with a simple framework from the research on trust in organizations. It suggests that trust typically develops through two main mechanisms: the creation of positive conditions that set the stage for easing another's sense of vulnerability and by entering into a series of successful social exchanges. When we apply the Bryk and Schneider (2002) theory of trust in schools to this framework, the social exchanges divide into low-risk exchanges that promote positive discernments of respect and personal regard and high-risk exchanges that promote positive discernments of competence and integrity. Thus, with the inclusion of the base conditions, there are three types of action in trust development: setting the stage for trust, creating opportunities for low-risk interactions, and creating opportunities for more high-risk interactions.

Using this framework, I then explored how the process might be promoted in schools. While mutual dependencies exist across all roles in schools, it is the principal who has the most power in the urban school community. Individual teachers are certainly in the position to build trust with parents and their colleagues, but they lack the formal authority to implement school policies that will make the growth of trust more likely throughout the entire school. A principal holds formal power over the teachers' positions and informal authority over low-income parents who lack an equal education or job status. In this atmosphere, it is incumbent upon the principal to reduce the vulnerabilities of others to initiate the growth of trust in the school. The principal is in the best position to bring participants together in low-risk and high-risk exchanges that promote positive discernments of respect, personal regard, competence, and integrity. An examination of the literature on principal leadership and school change provided insights on the practices that are linked with successful leadership for school reform. Among these practices were several that are likely to set the stage for the growth of trust, engage participants in low-risk exchanges that are likely to promote mutual respect and personal regard, and create opportunities for high-risk interactions that are likely to promote the exchange of positive discernments of competence and integrity. Case studies in this book provided illustrations of how these practices might help to build trust. Empirical analyses supported the research, providing further evidence that these practices should be guiding principles for school leadership. So let's take another look at what steps a principal can take to help build trust in schools.

Put Others at Ease

Communicating a belief system that promotes doing what is best for the children is a necessary precursor to the growth of trust in schools. If teachers believe that decisions are being made for the benefit of the children, they are more likely to put aside their own interests and support the work of the principal. The principals at all three case study schools put special emphasis on their efforts to convey a vision of schooling that put the needs of the students first. When talking about policy changes, each principal spoke in terms of doing what was best for the children. They also conveyed this vision in less direct ways. At MacNeil, Dr. Wilson walked through hallways, calling the children by name, asking about their classroom work, and talking to parents about other family members. At Cole Magnet, Mr. Truman greeted the children as they came from the school buses, asked about their homework, and talked to them about decorum. At Mills, Mrs. Munez made connections with children's families, helped set up nutrition classes for parents, and recruited parents to form a school safety patrol to escort students to and from school. The empirical analyses on low-trust schools found that communicating a vision was an effective mechanism for principals to build trust with teachers.

Remove Barriers to Trust

During the course of this study, it became clear that setting the stage for positive interactions involves putting people in a position where the development of trust is possible. Simply bringing people together to engage in social interactions does not guarantee positive perceptions of respect, personal regard, competence, and integrity. To ensure more positive outcomes, it is better to begin by assembling a group of people who are generally respectful, caring, and competent and who act with integrity. Therefore, one of the primary mechanisms for setting the stage for the growth of trust involves reshaping the faculty to eliminate divisive personalities and incompetent teachers.

The second case study school, Mills, is a strong example of a principal removing teachers who were barriers to the growth of trust in the school. At the time Mrs. Munez became principal, the school was immersed in the racial tensions that gripped the surrounding community. Many of the White faculty members had aligned themselves with community leaders who were fighting the influx of Hispanic families. These teachers not only ignored the needs of their Hispanic students, but also were openly hostile to their minority colleagues. During this time of racial strife, some incompetent teachers were allowed to remain on staff simply based on political beliefs rather than what was best for the students. Most decisions were made to further the battle against the Hispanic migration. Therefore, with a change in leadership, Mrs. Munez chose to remove many teachers to bring together a faculty that was open to building relationships with one another, their new principal, and the Hispanic families the school served.

The removal of problem faculty members not only results in a more cohesive group but also signals to others that the principal is dedicated to doing what is best for the students. The statistical analyses on low-trust schools demonstrates that reshaping the faculty is positively linked to the growth of teacher-principal trust. In these schools, teachers perceived that the principal was acting with competence and integrity by pushing out teachers who were incompetent or divisive, thereby allowing trust between teachers and school administrators to grow.

It is interesting to note that, like other policy changes, the faculty must perceive changes as part of an overall plan that will make things better for the students. Early in Mrs. Munez's tenure, the teachers accepted the drastic reshaping of the faculty at Mills as they witnessed oppositional teachers leaving and racial tensions in the school fading. However, as time went on and the faculty continued to be unstable, many teachers became uncomfortable with the principal's actions. Once they could no longer see the connection between the removal of teachers and meeting the needs of the children, some of the remaining teachers began to feel unsafe themselves. They perceived the principal's actions as serving her own interests rather than those of the children.

Provide Opportunities for People to Interact

Along with setting the stage for positive exchanges, the principal can create opportunities for successful interactions. Over the course of this book, I discussed how exchanges might be designed as low risk so that people might engage with one another while maintaining a low sense of vulnerability. Often, such low-risk exchanges are simply social in nature or involve work that is easily accomplished. These activities are designed to promote positive exchanges of respect and personal regard. Once low-risk exchanges are successfully underway, a principal may provide opportunities for high-risk exchanges that are likely to promote positive discernments of competence and integrity. Such interactions are often organized to allow faculty members to work together to make a school better. As I review the types of activities that might serve as opportunities for low- and high-risk interactions, I emphasize important insights from the literature and case studies.

Keep risks low when vulnerabilities are high. The literature on building trust suggests that when trust is low and, therefore, vulnerabilities are high, one must propose low-risk activities to engage people in interaction. When a new principal comes to a school, both teachers and parents have heightened feelings of vulnerability due to their lack of previous experience with the principal. They have no past knowledge to help them predict future behavior. In addition, the principal is in a position of power over them and their children. Even in schools that are not experiencing a change in leadership, the constant flow of students and parents through the school presents circumstances in which people with very little knowledge of one another must interact. As rates of student mobility between schools increase, teachers and administrators are faced with building relationships with larger groups of new parents and students each year. Even those parents who remain in a school community must begin new relationships with their children's teachers each year as their children progress through the grades. Thus, it is quite common for people to have heightened vulnerabilities in schools. As such, there is a constant need to provide opportunities for low-risk interactions.

As I discussed earlier, an easy first step in helping to promote the growth of positive relationships is to have people work together on easily accomplished projects. At MacNeil, Dr. Wilson brought parents, teachers, and students together to plant and maintain a community garden. Preparing a planting bed, pulling weeds, planting flowers, and installing a border were low-stress activities with a meaningful outcome. Those who participated could see their success at the end of the project and feel a sense of pride in a job well done. By joining in such projects, teachers and parents are brought together in an atmosphere that is likely to promote positive demonstrations of respect and personal regard.

The second method we examined for promoting low-risk exchanges involved using the small-group format for meetings to promote open discussion and encourage participation. Small-group committees were a successful tool for the principal at MacNeil. Dr. Wilson was able to enlist the help of a large number of faculty members to join committees in the school. Teachers on these committees approached their work with lively discussion and active participation. The small-group format made consensus easier to achieve. The positive energy generated at the committee level was then used to help projects gain momentum when brought to the school as a whole. For example, the school improvement plan committee was able to use the small-group format to outline areas for improvement, then present those areas to larger audiences, such as those at parent and faculty meetings, during which they hoped to receive feedback on their work and to recruit new members to the committee. Then they returned to the small-group format to draft the plan before presenting it for input and approval to the larger groups.

While extra projects and small-group work may help set a positive atmosphere in which people can interact, a principal can use everyday interactions with teachers and parents as opportunities to convey respect and personal regard. The same activities the principals in the cases used to convey their vision of schooling were also used to demonstrate respect and personal regard. While touring the school several times a day, Dr. Wilson took the time to speak with people she encountered in the hallway. Whether they were teachers, students, or parents, she greeted them warmly and talked to them briefly about either a personal interest of theirs or a school-related issue that they had discussed earlier. Similar opportunities arise for positive social interactions while in faculty meetings, in parent conferences, and in front of the school in the morning and at the end of the school day.

In part, by engaging in positive social interactions during everyday activities, the principal is setting a tone in the school of how others should interact. This modeling of appropriate behavior is especially powerful as an example to teachers of their expected behavior with parents. Some teachers at MacNeil talked of how they followed the principal's lead in using the time when parents dropped their children off in the morning and picked them up in the afternoon to form bonds with their students' families by saying hello, meeting other family members, and engaging in short conversations about the day's activities. While mostly social, the teachers felt that these conversations were important in helping them understand their students and in helping parents partner with them in educating the children.

Because everyday interactions often fall into a pattern of repeated exchanges of the same sort with the same people, special social events can help to break the pattern so that positive interaction might occur between individuals who do not typically see one another. Organizing these events to include fun activities helps people treat one another with respect and personal regard. The principal at Mills took teachers out to dinner. The principal at MacNeil organized bowling nights for teachers and holiday potluck dinners for parents and school staff. Even more, she talked to people one-on-one about these events quite often to encourage their attendance. In addition, empirical analysis showed low-risk social interaction to be effective in building teacher-teacher trust in low-trust schools.

Finally, as discussed in the case studies, the existence of a low base state of trust may require more investment of time in low-risk interactions. We saw how the principal at MacNeil, where trust was already high, was able to move quickly into high-risk interactions, while still providing opportunities for low-risk interactions. However, at Mills, Mrs. Munez concentrated her efforts on low-risk interactions to raise the trust level at the school from its extremely low state. In such a low-trust school, it would be difficult to immediately engage people in high-risk interaction with successful outcomes.

Add opportunities for high-risk interaction. In comparing Mills and MacNeil, we noted that Mrs. Munez invested her efforts in low-risk inter-actions. However, as discussed in the case studies, it is equally important to transition activities so that once trust relationships begin to develop, higher-risk interactions are introduced. Principals, teachers, and parents must move beyond mutual respect and personal regard to include positive perceptions of integrity and competence for trust to deepen. Developing a shared school mission or a strategic plan of action provides easy opportu-nities for administrators, teachers, and even parents to work together in ways that demonstrate their competence and integrity. During these dis-cussions, individuals may publicly express their personal values regarding schooling and how they enact those values in their teaching, school man-agement, or parenting. The process of coming to a consensus on a goal and how to get there helps people learn what they expect of each other. In addi-tion, it helps them to build positive perceptions of others' integrity when common goals are stated in terms of helping the children. In that a shared goal and strategic plan enables them to improve their own work and the work of the school in general, they also help individuals make positive discernments about one another's competence.

Create formal structures for both low- and high-risk interaction. While much of the work in building trust occurs during informal, one-on-one interac-tion, a principal can create formal structures that promote successful inter-actions. An obvious way to do this is by restructuring time and space. The principal at MacNeil scheduled common prep periods for teachers at the same grade level. She then worked to restructure the week so that teachers would have extra time during the school day to hold grade-level meetings. Teachers at MacNeil often talked about how important these schedule changes were to their ability to develop relationships based on working together. However, they also lamented that the school had no faculty lunch-room, which could help provide them with structured social time together. Although they had time to meet with one another in classrooms, they wanted a common social space for informal interaction across the faculty.

Teachers at Cole Magnet had multiple formal structures in place to pro-mote interactions. They held grade-level meetings and were each members of at least two committees. The committees were formed to address the sub-stantive areas of school improvement and real policy issues. As a result, the teachers at Cole Magnet were assured of one another's competence and integrity. They were aware of what was going on in their colleagues' classrooms and perceived that they were all dedicated to doing what was best for the children.

The development of consistent, formal home-school connections creates opportunities for structured interactions between the school staff and parents. Schools may use monthly newsletters with descriptions of classroom activities as a way to interact with parents. As at MacNeil, daily student agendas allow parents to become involved in the curriculum and to make judgments about the teachers' competence. In addition, the requirement of a parent's signature on the agenda gives feedback to the teacher that the parent is supportive of his or her child's education. Finally, creating parent seats on important school committees provides high-risk interactions in which both teacher and parent can make judgments of integrity and competence.

Beyond giving people time and space to interact, a principal can formalize interactions by giving people work to do together. Shared decision making offers a forum for trust development in that it requires high-risk interactions that center on improving the work of the school and involve increasing the technical and leadership skills of the teaching staff. In this sense, shared decision making promotes positive discernments of others' integrity and competence. However, if shared decision making is to succeed, there must already be some level of trust among the teachers. As such, shifting control is a mechanism for trust building that should be used after significant work has been done to ease vulnerabilities and build basic levels of trust.

Shared decision making is also a mechanism for building trust between a principal and teachers. When a principal shares authority with teachers, he or she eases the vulnerability that comes from the superior-subordinate relationship. The principal is treating the faculty as colleagues and partners in furthering the work of the school. In addition, by conferring some power to teachers, the principal is, in effect, taking the first risk in building trust. The principal is conveying to teachers that he or she perceives that they are competent and acting with integrity.

On the other hand, when a principal fails to share decision making with the faculty, the growth of trust may be limited. At Mills, the principal began her tenure facing extreme challenges from her faculty and community. She was forced to build a base of power and support system to set up the base conditions for trust building. However, even after a drastic reshaping of the faculty, she remained the sole authority in the school, failing to grant decision-making power on even mundane issues to faculty committees. As such, the teachers were wary of her authority and remained vulnerable subordinates.

Provide Guidance and Support for
Continued School Improvement

It appears from the case studies that, even when trust is high, a principal must provide leadership toward continued improvement to maintain the positive perceptions of competence and integrity between the teacher and principal and among teachers. Many teachers at Cole Magnet noted that Mr. Truman's style of leadership involved giving teachers freedom to govern both in their classrooms and through the established committee structure. While they talked of their sense of relief with this leadership after the more intrusive style of the previous principal, some worried that the school lacked momentum toward improvement. Teachers characterized their colleagues as highly competent, but most still expected the faculty to push themselves further—to be continuous learners. Some teachers felt that, even in a school that functioned well with shared governance, the principal should be the leader in setting a tone for continued improvement.

CONCLUSION

While it may not be surprising to those who work in schools that trust is an important part of any reform effort, we seldom create formal strategies to build relationships when implementing change. We often focus on best practices. Sometimes we tinker with organizational structure. Over time, we've heard of successes and failures with identical reform efforts. People and the relationships they maintain with one another are the key variables affecting the outcome.

This book presented a series of mechanisms that are useful in developing trust in a school community. Using research on trust in organizations as a guide, I suggested a model of trust building and linked the model to the policies and practices that principals can implement to encourage the growth of trust. The case studies and empirical analyses further illustrated how that model might operate within differing school contexts. What we have now is a blueprint for trust building. Let's continue to uncover the details as we go about the business of improving our schools.

Resource A

CCSR Relational Trust Measures

While the Consortium attempted to survey all teachers and principals in the Chicago public school system, they put extra effort into data collection from a probability school sample, stratified by school neighborhood. Once the data were collected, the Consortium conducted a nonresponse bias analysis based on teachers' race, gender, years of teaching experience, and highest degree earned and the percentage of low-income students in the school. Comparing the sample to the universe of Chicago public schools, no response bias was found in either year of data collection. In addition, the Consortium compared the probability sample with the characteristics of the volunteer respondents (those not in the sample) and found that the two groups were similar. Over the years in working with their survey data, the Consortium has identified a group of high-achieving schools that are atypical of Chicago public schools. Data from these 40 schools inappropriately skews results so that variance among the other 450 schools is muddled. Typically, these schools are removed from studies at the Consortium to gain a better understanding of what is happening in the vast majority of the schools. In this study, I followed the example of the Consortium and used data from both the volunteer and analytic samples except for the top 40, historically high-achieving schools.

In 1997, 422 of the system's 477 elementary schools participated in either or both the teacher and student surveys. Sixty-three percent of elementary school teachers and 83% of principals responded to the survey (King-Bilcer, 1997). In 1999, 76% or 378 of 498 elementary schools participated in the survey. The respondents included 263 (53%) principals and 7,905 (52%) elementary school teachers (Hart, 2000).

The measures of relational trust used in this study, along with many of the CCSR measures that represented mechanisms for building trust, were created by analysts at the Consortium using Rasch Rating Scale Analysis

(Wright & Masters, 1982). The Rasch model is an item-response, latent-trait model. The set of survey items in a measure are first used to define a scale of item difficulty based on the relative probability of a respondent choosing each category on each item. Individuals are then placed on this scale based on their particular responses to the items in the measure. The scale units are logits.

Rasch analysis produces three types of statistics. The first is item difficulty, which estimates the likelihood that respondents will endorse the position, attitude, or behavior represented by each item within a scale. For example, common events, attitudes, and beliefs are *less difficult* to endorse; rarer ones are *more difficult*. Second is item infit, which is the degree to which individuals respond to a particular item consistent with its placement in a hierarchically ordered scale. For a properly fitting item, individuals who endorse that item are more likely to endorse the easier, less difficult items below it in the scale and are not as likely to endorse the items that are harder or more difficult and above it in the scale. Third is person reliability, which is a measure of the internal consistency of the scale items and is similar to Cronbach's alpha.

Survey items are grouped to form a measure based on the concept the analysts are attempting to capture. However, in fitting the Rasch model, some items may statistically misfit, and barring strong conceptual reasons to the contrary, they are removed from the measure. CCSR then produces school-level means by aggregating individual responses while weighting by the inverse of the standard error.

Table A.1   Rasch Scale of 1997 Teacher-Principal Trust

Teacher-Principal Trust		Measure Reliability: 0.92
Item	Difficulty	Infit
*It's okay in this school to discuss feelings, worries, and frustrations with the principal.[a]	0.79	0.91
*The principal looks out for the personal welfare of the faculty members.[a]	0.33	0.84
*I trust the principal at his or her word.[a]	0.21	0.84
The principal at this school is an effective manager who makes the school run smoothly.[a]	0.05	1.16
The principal places the needs of children ahead of his or her personal and political interests.[a]	−0.02	1.09
*The principal has confidence in the expertise of the teachers.[a]	−0.17	1.14
*The principal takes a personal interest in the professional development of teachers.[a]	−0.20	0.91
I really respect my principal as an educator.[a]	−0.27	0.85
*To what extent do you feel respected by your principal?[c]	−0.73	1.22

SOURCE: *Public Use Data Set User's Manual,* copyright © 1999, Consortium on Chicago School Research. Used with permission.

NOTE:

a Four-point scale: *Strongly Disagree; Disagree; Agree; Strongly Agree*
b Five-point scale: *None; Some; About Half; Most; Nearly All*
c Four-point scale: *Not at All; A Little; Some; To a Great Extent*
* Item used in 1994 measure

Table A.2 Rasch Scale of 1997 Teacher-Teacher Trust

Teacher-Teacher Trust	Measure Reliability: 0.82	
Item	Difficulty	Infit
*How many teachers in this school really care about each other?[b]	2.31	1.03
*Teachers in this school trust each other.[a]	1.01	0.72
*It's okay in this school to discuss feelings, worries, and frustrations with other teachers.[a]	0.34	1.00
*Teachers respect other teachers who take the lead in school improvement efforts.[a]	−0.12	0.90
Teachers at this school respect those colleagues who are expert at their craft.[a]	−1.12	0.99
*To what extent do you feel respected by other teachers?[c]	−2.42	1.32

SOURCE: *Public Use Data Set User's Manual,* copyright © 1999, Consortium on Chicago School Research. Used with permission.

NOTE: The 1994 measure also included "Most teachers in this school are cordial."
a Four-point scale: *Strongly Disagree; Disagree; Agree; Strongly Agree*
b Five-point scale: *None; Some; About Half; Most; Nearly All*
c Four-point scale: *Not at All; A Little; Some; To a Great Extent*
* Item used in 1994 measure

Table A.3   Rasch Scale of 1997 Teacher-Parent Trust

Teacher-Parent Trust	Measure Reliability: 0.78	
Item	Difficulty	Infit
How many of your students' parents do their best to help their children learn?[b]	1.83	1.12
*How many teachers at this school feel good about parents' support for their work?[b]	1.59	1.03
*How many teachers at this school really care about this local community?[b]	1.48	1.14
How many of your students' parents support your teaching efforts?[b]	0.90	1.05
Teachers and parents think of each other as partners in educating children.[a]	0.73	0.87
[R]At this school, it is difficult to overcome the cultural barriers between teachers and parents.[a]	−0.02	1.36
*Parents have confidence in the expertise of the teachers.[a]	−0.11	0.81
[R]There is conflict between parents and teachers at this school.[a]	−0.21	1.05
*Staff at this school work hard to build trusting relationships with parents.[a]	−0.41	0.81
Talking with parents helps me understand my students better.[a]	−1.23	1.20
*To what extent do teachers in this school respect parents and members of the local community?[c]	−1.39	0.84
*To what extent do teachers in this school respect students' parents?[c]	−1.55	0.79
*To what extent do you feel respected by the parents of your students?[c]	−1.61	0.85

SOURCE: *Public Use Data Set User's Manual,* copyright © 1999, Consortium on Chicago School Research. Used with permission.

NOTE:

a Four-point scale: *Strongly Disagree; Disagree; Agree; Strongly Agree*
b Five-point scale: *None; Some; About Half; Most; Nearly All*
c Four-point scale: *Not at All; A Little; Some; To a Great Extent*
* Item used in 1994 measure
R Item was reversed for analysis purposes.

Table A.4   Rasch Scale of 1999 Teacher-Principal Trust

Teacher-Principal Trust	Measure Reliability: 0.89	
Item	Difficulty	Infit
*It's okay in this school to discuss feelings, worries, and frustrations with the principal.[a]	0.79	0.87
*The principal looks out for the personal welfare of the faculty members.[a]	0.33	0.79
*I trust the principal at his or her word.[a]	0.21	0.70
The principal at this school is an effective manager who makes the school run smoothly.[a]	0.05	1.14
The principal places the needs of children ahead of his or her personal and political interests.[a]	−0.02	1.03
*The principal has confidence in the expertise of the teachers.[a]	−0.17	0.93
*The principal takes a personal interest in the professional development of teachers.[a]	−0.20	0.88
*To what extent do you feel respected by your principal?[c]	−0.73	0.96

SOURCE: *Public Use Data Set User's Manual,* copyright © 1999, Consortium on Chicago School Research. Used with permission.

NOTE:
a Four-point scale: *Strongly Disagree; Disagree; Agree; Strongly Agree*
b Five-point scale: *None; Some; About Half; Most; Nearly All*
c Four-point scale: *Not at All; A Little; Some; To a Great Extent*
*Item used in 1994 measure

Table A.5   Rasch Scale of 1999 Teacher-Teacher Trust

Teacher-Teacher Trust	Measure Reliability: 0.82	
Item	Difficulty	Infit
*How many teachers in this school really care about each other?[b]	2.31	1.04
*Teachers in this school trust each other.[a]	1.01	0.63
*It's okay in this school to discuss feelings, worries, and frustrations with other teachers.[a]	0.34	0.94
*Teachers respect other teachers who take the lead in school improvement efforts.[a]	−0.12	0.83
Teachers at this school respect those colleagues who are expert at their craft.[a]	−1.12	0.93
*To what extent do you feel respected by other teachers?[c]	−2.42	1.22

SOURCE: *Public Use Data Set User's Manual,* copyright © 1999, Consortium on Chicago School Research. Used with permission.

NOTE: The 1994 measure also included "Most teachers in this school are cordial."
a Four-point scale: *Strongly Disagree; Disagree; Agree; Strongly Agree*
b Five-point scale: *None; Some; About Half; Most; Nearly All*
c Four-point scale: *Not at All; A Little; Some; To a Great Extent*
*Item used in 1994 measure

Table A.6   Rasch Scale of 1999 Teacher-Parent Trust

Teacher-Parent Trust	Measure Reliability: 0.58	
Item	Difficulty	Infit
How many of your students' parents do their best to help their children learn?[b]	1.83	0.79
*How many teachers at this school feel good about parents' support for their work?[b]	1.59	0.93
How many of your students' parents support your teaching efforts?[b]	0.90	0.86
Teachers and parents think of each other as partners in educating children.[a]	0.73	0.83
[R]At this school, it is difficult to overcome the cultural barriers between teachers and parents.[a]	−0.02	1.70
*Parents have confidence in the expertise of the teachers.[a]	−0.11	0.68
*Staff at this school work hard to build trusting relationships with parents.[a]	−0.41	0.89
*To what extent do you feel respected by the parents of your students?[c]	−1.61	0.43

SOURCE: *Public Use Data Set User's Manual,* copyright © 1999, Consortium on Chicago School Research. Used with permission.

NOTE:
a Four-point scale: *Strongly Disagree; Disagree; Agree; Strongly Agree*
b Five-point scale: *None; Some; About Half; Most; Nearly All*
c Four-point scale: *Not at All; A Little; Some; To a Great Extent*
*Item used in 1994 measure
R Item was reversed for analysis purposes.

Resource B

Measures of Key Concepts of Trust Building

NOTE: (T) = Teacher response measure or items
(P) = Principal response measure or items
(R) = Item reversed for statistical analysis

SETTING THE STAGE

Principal Has the Ability to Reshape the Faculty (P)

CCSR Rasch Measure HRDE

Please rate the extent to which the following have changed in the past two years:

_____ Responsiveness of staff development to teachers' needs

_____ My autonomy in selecting teachers for this school

_____ Ease in getting new staff hired

_____ Effectiveness of teacher remediation procedures for improving teaching

_____ Ease in removing nonperforming teachers

Response Scale: *Worse; No Change; Better*

Principal Articulates a Belief System Around Doing What Is Best for the Children (T)

CCSR Rasch Measure INST

Please mark the extent to which you agree or disagree with each of the following:

The principal at this school:

_____ Carefully tracks student academic progress.

_____ Understands how children learn.

_____ Presses teachers to implement what they have learned in professional development.

_____ Communicates a clear vision for our school.

_____ Sets high standards for student learning.

_____ Sets high standards for teaching.

_____ Makes clear to staff his or her expectations for meeting instructional goals.

Response Scale: *Strongly Disagree; Disagree; Agree; Strongly Agree*

SUCCESSFUL SIMPLE SOCIAL INTERACTIONS

Informal Interactions Among Teachers (T)

Please mark the extent to which you agree or disagree with each of the following:

_____ Most teachers in this school are cordial.

_____ Teachers in this school share and discuss student work with other teachers.

Response Scale: *Strongly Disagree; Disagree; Agree; Strongly Agree*

Informal Interactions Between School Staff and Parents (T)

Please mark the extent to which you agree or disagree with the following:

_____ Parents are greeted warmly when they call or visit the school.

Response Scale: *Strongly Disagree; Disagree; Agree; Strongly Agree*

Principal Models Behavior With Parents (T)

Please mark the extent to which you agree or disagree with each of the following:

The principal at this school:

_____ Pushes teachers to communicate regularly with parents.

_____ Promotes parent and community involvement in the school.

Response Scale: *Strongly Disagree; Disagree; Agree; Strongly Agree*

Teacher-Parent Social Events (T)

For the students you teach this year, how many of their parents:

_____ Attended schoolwide special events?

_____ (R) Didn't show up for school events and conferences intended for them?

Response Scale: *None; Some; About Half; Most; Nearly All*

SUCCESSFUL COMPLEX INTERACTIONS

School Outreach to Parents (T)

Please mark the extent to which you agree or disagree with each of the following:

_____ Parents are invited to visit classrooms to observe the instructional program.

_____ We encourage feedback from parents and the community.

_____ Teachers work closely with parents to meet students' needs.

_____ We work at communicating to parents about support needed to advance the school mission.

_____ This school regularly communicates with parents about how they can help their children learn.

Response Scale: *Strongly Disagree; Disagree; Agree; Strongly Agree*

Parents Volunteer at the School (T)

For the students you teach this year, how many of their parents:

_____ Helped raise funds for the school?

_____ Volunteered to help in the classroom?

Response Scale: *None; Some; About Half; Most; Nearly All*

Teachers Do Problem Solving Together (T)

CCSR Rasch Measure PBSV

Please mark the extent to which you agree or disagree with each of the following:

_____ Faculty meetings are often used for problem solving.

_____ The faculty has a good process for making group decisions and/or solving problems.

_____ Many teachers express their personal views at faculty meetings.

_____ We do a good job of talking through views, opinions, and values.

_____ (R) When a conflict arises, we usually "sweep it under the rug."

Response Scale: *Strongly Disagree; Disagree; Agree; Strongly Agree*

Teachers Reflect on Teaching Together (T)

This school year, how often have you had conversations with colleagues about:

_____ The goals of this school?

_____ Development of new curriculum?

_____ Managing classroom behavior?

_____ What helps students learn best?

Response Scale: *Less Than Once a Month; Two or Three Times a Month; Once or Twice a Week; Almost Daily*

Please mark the extent to which you agree or disagree with each of the following:

_____ Teachers in this school regularly discuss assumptions about teaching and learning.

_____ Teachers talk about instruction in the teachers' lounge, faculty meetings, and so on.

Response Scale: *Strongly Disagree; Disagree; Agree; Strongly Agree*

Teachers Share in a School
Mission That Puts Children First (T, P)

Please mark the extent to which you agree or disagree with each of the following:

_____ Teachers work together to do what is best for the kids.

_____ Teachers take responsibility for improving the school.

_____ Teachers set high standards for themselves.

_____ Teachers feel responsible to help each other do their best.

_____ Teachers feel responsible for all students to learn.

_____ Teachers feel responsible when students in this school fail.

Response Scale: *Strongly Disagree; Disagree; Agree; Strongly Agree*

Pursuing a Plan of Strategic Action (T)

Please mark the extent to which you agree or disagree with each of the following:

_____ Teachers design instructional programs together.

_____ Teachers at this school make a conscious effort to coordinate their teaching with instruction at other grade levels.

Response Scale: *Strongly Disagree; Disagree; Agree; Strongly Agree*

Teachers Work on Developing an Instructional Program Together (T)

CCSR Rasch Measure SLRN

Please mark the extent to which you agree or disagree with each of the following:

_____ This school really works at developing students' social skills.

_____ When making important decisions, the school always focuses on what's best for student learning.

_____ This school has well-defined learning expectations for all students.

_____ This school sets high standards for academic performance.

_____ The school day is organized to maximize instructional time.

Response Scale: *Strongly Disagree; Disagree; Agree; Strongly Agree*

Teachers Share in the Decision Making (T)

CCSR Rasch Measure INFL

How much influence do teachers have over school policy in each of the areas below?

_____ Hiring new professional personnel

_____ Hiring a new principal

_____ Determining the school's schedule (including teacher preparation periods)

_____ Planning how discretionary school funds should be used

_____ Determining specific professional and teaching assignments

_____ Determining the content of inservice programs

_____ Setting standards for student behavior

_____ Establishing the curriculum and instructional program

_____ Determining how students' progress is measured

_____ Determining books and other instructional materials used in classrooms

Response Scale: *None; A Little; Some; A Great Deal*

Please mark the extent to which you disagree or agree with each of the following:

_____ Teachers are involved in making the important decisions in this school.

_____ Teachers have a lot of informal opportunities to influence what happens here.

_____ I feel comfortable voicing my concerns in this school.

Response Scale: *Strongly Disagree; Disagree; Agree; Strongly Agree*

Buffer Principal (T/P)

(T) Please mark the extent to which you disagree or agree with the following:

_____ Principal promotes parent and community involvement.

Response Scale: *Strongly Disagree; Disagree; Agree; Strongly Agree*

(T) Please rate the extent to which the following have changed in the past two years in your school:

_____ The school's relations with parents

_____ How the school relates to the community

Response Scale: *Worse; No Change; Better*

(P) Please indicate the extent to which the following may be a factor in preventing your school from improving:

_____ Mistrust between teachers and parents

Response Scale: *Not a Factor; Somewhat a Factor; Serious Factor*

Parent Involvement (T)

CCSR Rasch Measure PART

For the students you teach this year, how many of their parents:

_____ Attended parent-teacher conferences when you requested them?

_____ Helped raise funds for the school?

_____ Volunteered to help in the classroom?

_____ Picked up their child's last report card?

_____ Attended schoolwide special events?

_____ Didn't show up for school events and conferences intended for them?

Response Scale: *None; Some; About Half; Most; Nearly All*

OTHER VARIABLES USED IN THE ANALYSES

Predominately African American 1999 is a dummy variable that is coded 1 if the percentage of African American students in the school is greater than 85%.

Predominately Hispanic 1999 is a dummy variable that is coded 1 if the percentage of Hispanic students in the school is greater than 85.

Predominately Minority 1999 is a dummy variable that is coded 1 if more than 85% of the student body is a mixed minority.

Racially Mixed 1999 is a dummy variable that is coded 1 if between 15 and 30% of the student body is White.

Integrated Student Body 1999 is a dummy variable that is coded 1 if 30% or more of the students in the school are White. This variable is the eliminated category in the analysis.

Concentration of Poverty is a composite measure created from 1990 U.S. Census statistics for each school's census block. It consists of two pieces of information: the percentage of males over twenty-one years of age who are employed and the percentage of families above the poverty line. These are reverse-coded to transfer the variable into a concentration of poverty indicator.

Small School 1999 is a dummy variable that is coded 1 if the number of students enrolled in the school in 1993 was less than 350.

Prior Achievement 1989 is the log of the mean value of the school's 1988–1989 Illinois Goal Assessment Program (IGAP) scores in third-, sixth-, and eighth-grade reading and mathematics.

References

Batenburg, R., Raub, W., & Snijders, C. (1997). *Contacts and contracts: Temporal embeddedness and the contractual behavior of firms.* Pionier Seminar, Utrecht, The Netherlands: Heidelberglaan.

Bidwell, C. E. (1970). Students and schools: Some observations on client trust in client-serving organizations. In W. R. Rosengren & M. Lefton (Eds.), *Organizations and clients: Essays in the sociology of service* (pp. 37-69). Columbus, OH: Merrill.

Blau, P. (1986). *Exchange and power in social life.* New York: Wiley.

Bryk, A. S., Lee, V. E., & Holland, P. B. (1993). *Catholic schools and the common good.* Cambridge, MA: Harvard University Press.

Bryk, A. S., & Schneider, B. (1996). *Social trust: A moral resource for school improvement.* Chicago: Consortium on Chicago School Research.

Bryk, A. S., & Schneider, B. (2002). *Trust in schools: A core resource for improvement.* New York: Russell Sage.

Bryk, A. S., Sebring, P. B., Kerbow, D., Rollow, S., & Easton, J. Q. (1998). *Charting Chicago school reform: Democratic localism as a lever for change.* Boulder, CO: Westview Press.

Comer, J. P., & Haynes, N. M. (1999). The dynamics of school change: Response to the article "Comer's school development program in Prince George's County, Maryland: A theory-based evaluation" by Thomas D. Cook et al. *American Educational Research Journal, 36*(3), 599-608.

Deal, T. E., & Peterson, K. D. (1994). *The leadership paradox: Balancing logic and artistry in schools.* San Francisco: Jossey-Bass.

Elmore, R. F., Peterson, P. L., & McCarthey, S. J. (1996). *Restructuring the classroom.* San Francisco: Jossey-Bass.

Fine, G. A., & Holyfield, L. (1996). Secrecy, trust, and dangerous leisure: Generating group cohesion in voluntary organizations. *Social Psychology Quarterly, 59*(1), 22-38.

Goddard, R. D., Tschannen-Moran, M., & Hoy, W. (2001). A multi-level examination of the distribution and effects of teacher trust in students and parents in urban elementary schools. *Elementary School Journal, 102*(1), 3-19.

Grossman, P. (1992). In pursuit of a dual agenda: Creating a middle-level professional development school. In L. Darling-Hammond (Ed.), *Professional development schools: Schools for developing a profession* (pp. 50-73). New York: Teachers College Press.

Gulati, R. (1995). Does familiarity breed trust? The implications of repeated ties for contractual choice in alliances. *Academy of Management Journal, 38,* 85-112.

Hart, H. (2000). *Public use data set user's manual for improving Chicago's schools: The teacher's turn, 1999.* Chicago: Consortium on Chicago School Research.

Hoy, W. K., Tarter, C. J., & Witkoskie, L. (1992). Faculty trust in colleagues: Linking the principal with school effectiveness. *Journal of Research and Development in Education, 26*(1), 38-45.

Hoy, W. K., & Tschannen-Moran, M. (1999). Five faces of trust: An empirical confirmation in urban elementary schools. *Journal of School Leadership, 9,* 184-208.

King-Bilcer, D. (1997). *User's manual, version 1 for improving Chicago's schools: The teacher's turn, 1997.* Chicago: Consortium on Chicago School Research.

Lareau, A. (1989). *Home advantage: Social class and parental intervention in elementary education.* New York: Falmer Press.

Leithwood, K. (1994). Leadership for school restructuring. *Educational Administration Quarterly, 30*(4), 498-518.

Levitt, B., & March, J. G. (1988). Organizational learning. *Annual Review of Sociology, 14,* 319-340.

Lewicki, R. J., & Bunker, B. B. (1995). Trust in relationships: A model of development and decline. In B. B. Bunker, J. Z. Rubin, & Associates (Eds.), *Conflict, cooperation, and justice: Essays inspired by the work of Morton Deutsch* (pp. 133-173). San Francisco: Jossey-Bass.

Louis, K. S., & Kruse, S. D. (1995). *Professionalism and community: Perspectives on reforming urban schools.* Thousand Oaks, CA: Corwin.

Louis, K. S., & Miles, M. B. (1990). *Improving the urban high school: What works and why.* New York: Teachers College Press.

Macneil, I. (1985). Relational contract: What we do and do not know. *Wisconsin Law Review, 3,* 483-526.

Mayer, R. C., Davis, J. H., & Schoorman, F. D. (1995). An integrative model of organizational trust. *Academy of Management Review, 20*(3), 709-734.

Meier, D. (1995). *The power of their ideas: Lessons for America from a small school in Harlem.* Boston, MA: Beacon Press.

Meier, D. (2002). *In schools we trust.* Boston: Beacon Press.

Meyer, J. W., & Rowan, B. (1977). Institutionalized organizations: Formal structure as myth and ceremony. *American Journal of Sociology, 83*(2), 340-363.

Miles, R. E., & Creed, W. E. D. (1995). Organizational forms and managerial philosophies: A descriptive and analytical review. *Research in Organizational Behavior, 17,* 333-372.

Muncey, D., & McQuillan, P. (1996). *Reform and resistance in schools and classrooms.* New Haven, CT: Yale University Press.

Newmann, F. M., & Associates. (1996). *Authentic achievement: Restructuring schools for intellectual quality.* San Francisco: Jossey-Bass.

Okun, A. (1981). *Prices and quantities.* Washington, DC: The Brookings Institution.

Ouchi, W. G. (1980). Markets, bureaucracies, and clans. *Administrative Science Quarterly, 25,* 129-141.

Powell, W. W. (1990). Neither market nor hierarchy: Network forms of organization. *Research in Organizational Behavior, 12,* 295-336.

Ring, P. S., & Van de Ven, A. H. (1994). Developmental processes of cooperative interorganizational relationships. *Academy of Management Review, 19*(1), 90-118.

Rousseau, D. M., & Parks, J. M. (1992). The contracts of individuals and organizations. *Research in Organizational Behavior, 15,* 1-43.

Sebring, P. B., Bryk, A. S., Easton, J. Q., Luppescu, S. S., Thum, S., Lopez, W., & Smith, B. (1995). *Charting reform: Chicago teachers take stock.* Chicago: Consortium on Chicago School Research.

Sergiovanni, T. J. (1992). *Moral leadership: Getting to the heart of school improvement.* San Francisco: Jossey-Bass.

Sergiovanni, T. J. (1994). *Building community in schools.* San Francisco: Jossey-Bass.

Spillane, J. P., & Thompson, C. L. (1997). Reconstructing conceptions of local capacity: The local education agency's capacity for ambitious instructional reform. *Education Evaluation and Policy Analysis, 19*(2), 185-203.

Tarter, C. J., Bliss, J. R., & Hoy, W. (1989). School characteristics and faculty trust in secondary schools. *Educational Administration Quarterly, 25*(3), 294-308.

Tarter, C. J., Sabo, D., & Hoy, W. (1995). Middle school climate, faculty trust, and effectiveness: A path analysis. *Journal of Research and Development in Education, 29*(1), 41-49.

Tschannen-Moran, M., & Hoy, W. (1998). Trust in schools: A conceptual and empirical analysis. *Journal of Educational Administration, 36*(4), 334-352.

Valdes, G. (1996). *Con respecto: Bridging the distance between culturally diverse families and schools.* New York: Teachers College Press.

Wong, K. K. (1990). *City choices: Education and housing.* Albany: State University of New York Press.

Wright, B. D., & Masters, G. N. (1982). *Rating scale analysis.* Chicago: Mesa Press.

Zucker, L. G. (1986). Production of trust: Institutional sources of economic structure, 1840–1920. *Research in Organizational Behavior, 8,* 53-111.

Index

CORWIN PRESS

The Corwin Press logo—a raven striding across an open book—represents the union of courage and learning. Corwin Press is committed to improving education for all learners by publishing books and other professional development resources for those serving the field of K–12 education. By providing practical, hands-on materials, Corwin Press continues to carry out the promise of its motto: **"Helping Educators Do Their Work Better."**